All About Bermuda Triangle: A Kid's Guide to the Mystery of the Atlantic

Educational Books For Kids, Volume 15

Shah Rukh

Published by Shah Rukh, 2024.

ALL ABOUT BERMUDA TRIANGLE: A KID'S GUIDE TO THE MYSTERY OF THE ATLANTIC

First edition. September 22, 2024.

Copyright © 2024 Shah Rukh.

ISBN: 979-8227169594

Written by Shah Rukh.

Table of Contents

Prologue

Welcome to the mysterious world of the Bermuda Triangle, a place where the ocean dances with secrets and adventures await at every turn! Stretching between Miami, Bermuda, and Puerto Rico, this enigmatic area of the Atlantic Ocean has captured the imaginations of explorers, scientists, and dreamers for centuries. But what makes the Bermuda Triangle so fascinating?

In this book, we'll dive deep into the stories of vanished ships, lost aircraft, and strange phenomena that have puzzled people for generations. You'll discover real-life mysteries, from the legendary disappearance of Flight 19 to the ghostly tales of the Mary Celeste. We'll explore the science behind the stories, uncovering the geography and natural wonders of this incredible region.

Each chapter will take you on a journey filled with adventure, wonder, and a little bit of spookiness. Whether you're a curious kid who loves mysteries or just someone who enjoys a good story, you're in the right place. So, grab your compass, put on your explorer's hat, and get ready to uncover the truth about the Bermuda Triangle—where the ocean hides its deepest secrets and the adventure is just beginning!

Chapter 1: The Disappearance of Flight 19

Flight 19 is one of the most mysterious and well-known incidents associated with the Bermuda Triangle, a region in the western part of the North Atlantic Ocean where ships and planes have reportedly vanished under mysterious circumstances. The disappearance of Flight 19 happened on December 5, 1945, just a few months after World War II had ended. Flight 19 was a group of five U.S. Navy torpedo bombers known as TBM Avengers, which took off from Naval Air Station Fort Lauderdale in Florida on what was supposed to be a routine training mission. The flight was led by an experienced instructor, Lieutenant Charles C. Taylor, and was composed of 14 airmen in total.

The mission for Flight 19 was simple: it was supposed to fly east from Fort Lauderdale over the Atlantic Ocean to conduct a bombing practice at a small island known as Hens and Chickens Shoals, then head north for a short distance before turning back to base. The entire exercise was expected to take about two hours. The weather at the time of departure was reported as favorable for flying, though there were some scattered clouds and light winds.

Things seemed to be going as planned until something went terribly wrong. A few hours into the mission, Lieutenant Taylor reported that his compass was malfunctioning and that he was disoriented. He believed that they were flying over the Florida Keys, a chain of islands southwest of Florida, when in fact they were much farther north, somewhere over the Atlantic Ocean. This error in navigation became critical as the flight group was flying farther and farther away from land, heading into the open ocean rather than toward the mainland. Taylor's sense of direction was failing him, and he was unable to determine the exact position of his squadron. The other pilots, being less experienced, trusted Taylor's judgment and followed his instructions, even though they were increasingly unsure about their location.

As time passed, the situation grew more desperate. Radio transmissions between the pilots and ground control at the naval station revealed growing confusion and panic. Taylor's messages to the ground became more frantic as he repeatedly stated that his compasses were malfunctioning and that the squadron was lost. He instructed his flight to fly northeast, believing they were off course and over the Gulf of Mexico. However, ground controllers believed they were actually over the Atlantic Ocean, east of Florida. Unfortunately, communication with the planes was intermittent and poor, partly due to static interference and possibly because of the distance the planes had traveled. Ground control advised Taylor to turn west, but for reasons that are still unclear, Taylor decided to continue flying east, which only took them further away from land and deeper into the Atlantic.

As night fell, the weather worsened, and the planes began to run low on fuel. Despite attempts from ground control to direct them back to safety, the squadron's last known position was somewhere near the vast stretch of water known as the Bermuda Triangle. The final radio communications from Flight 19 were disjointed and confusing. One of the last messages from Taylor indicated that both of his compasses were not functioning, and they had no idea where they were. Some reports suggest that Taylor was considering ditching the planes into the ocean once fuel ran out. Eventually, all contact with Flight 19 was lost, and the planes vanished without a trace.

Following the disappearance of Flight 19, the U.S. Navy launched an extensive search-and-rescue mission, deploying hundreds of aircraft, ships, and personnel to scour the area where the planes were last known to be. Oddly enough, one of the rescue planes, a PBM Mariner flying boat, also disappeared shortly after takeoff while searching for the missing planes. The Mariner and its 13 crew members were never found, adding another layer of mystery to the tragedy. For days, the search continued, but no trace of Flight 19 or the rescue plane was ever found. There was no wreckage, no oil slick, no debris—nothing.

The disappearance of Flight 19 has since become one of the most famous incidents associated with the Bermuda Triangle, and it has fueled countless theories about what happened that day. Some suggest that the planes may have encountered an unusual weather phenomenon, such as a sudden storm or waterspout, that caused them to crash into the ocean. Others believe that the compasses on the planes could have been affected by a magnetic anomaly in the Bermuda Triangle, leading to navigational errors. There are also theories that propose more far-fetched ideas, including alien abduction or the planes being swallowed by a vortex to another dimension.

One of the official explanations from the U.S. Navy's investigation into the disappearance of Flight 19 was that the planes likely ran out of fuel and crashed into the ocean, but the lack of any wreckage has kept speculation alive for decades. Some have pointed out that the area where Flight 19 was last believed to be is known for its deep waters, which could explain why no debris or wreckage has ever been found. The ocean floor in this part of the Atlantic is uneven and full of deep trenches, making it difficult to locate sunken planes. Additionally, the strong currents in the area could have quickly dispersed any floating debris, further complicating search efforts.

Another factor that has contributed to the enduring mystery is the leadership of Lieutenant Taylor. Though Taylor was an experienced pilot, his disorientation and confusion during the mission were evident in the radio transmissions. Some speculate that his insistence on flying east, rather than west as ground control advised, may have been due to spatial disorientation—a condition in which a pilot becomes confused about their position in the sky, especially when flying over water where there are no landmarks or visible horizons to guide them. However, there are still many who question why Taylor's instruments failed or why he believed he was over the Florida Keys when he was, in fact, over the Atlantic.

Despite the various explanations that have been proposed, the disappearance of Flight 19 remains unsolved. The mystery has captivated the imaginations of many and has been the subject of numerous books, documentaries, and even fictional stories. It is often cited as one of the key events that contribute to the legend of the Bermuda Triangle, a place where ships and planes seem to vanish under strange and unexplained circumstances. The story of Flight 19 continues to intrigue people around the world, not only because of the tragic loss of life but also because of the sense of the unknown that surrounds the incident.

Even today, the fate of Flight 19 is a topic of speculation. With advancements in technology, such as underwater drones and better sonar equipment, there have been renewed efforts to search for the missing planes, though none have been successful so far. The absence of any concrete evidence has allowed the mystery to persist, and the story of Flight 19 remains one of the most iconic unsolved disappearances in aviation history. For those who are fascinated by the Bermuda Triangle, the tale of Flight 19 serves as a chilling reminder of the strange and unexplained events that continue to haunt this region of the Atlantic.

Chapter 2: The Mystery of the Mary Celeste

The mystery of the Mary Celeste is one of the most enduring maritime mysteries in history, captivating the imagination of sailors, historians, and the general public for over a century. The Mary Celeste was a merchant brigantine, a type of ship that was commonly used in the 19th century for transporting goods across the oceans. On December 4, 1872, the Mary Celeste was discovered adrift in the Atlantic Ocean, completely deserted by her crew. What made this discovery so strange was that the ship was still seaworthy, with all its sails set and cargo intact, yet there was no sign of the captain, crew, or any of the people who had been aboard. This eerie abandonment, combined with the fact that no one ever saw the crew again, gave rise to one of the most famous unsolved mysteries in maritime history.

The Mary Celeste was built in 1861 in Nova Scotia, Canada, originally named the Amazon. After a few uneventful years of service, the ship encountered a series of mishaps, including several collisions and the death of her first captain due to illness. Eventually, the ship was sold to American owners, who renamed her the Mary Celeste. The ship was rigged as a brigantine and, after a major refit, resumed her role in transatlantic trade. In November 1872, she set sail from New York City under the command of Captain Benjamin Briggs, a respected and experienced mariner. Aboard were his wife, Sarah, their two-year-old daughter, Sophia, and a crew of seven men, all of whom were described as capable sailors.

The Mary Celeste was bound for Genoa, Italy, carrying a cargo of 1,701 barrels of denatured alcohol, a type of industrial-grade alcohol used primarily as a solvent or fuel. The voyage began without incident, and Captain Briggs had high hopes for a safe and successful journey. However, less than a month later, the ship was discovered adrift by the Dei Gratia, a British brig captained by David Morehouse, who coincidentally knew Briggs. Morehouse was puzzled when his crew spotted the Mary Celeste, as she appeared to be moving erratically and none of her crew could be seen on deck. Morehouse ordered his crew to investigate, fearing that the ship might be in distress.

When the crew of the Dei Gratia boarded the Mary Celeste, they were astonished to find the ship completely deserted. The last entry in the ship's logbook was dated ten days earlier, on November 25, 1872, and there were no signs of struggle or foul play. The ship's cargo of alcohol was mostly intact, with only a few barrels reportedly found empty. The personal belongings of the crew, including valuable items like Captain Briggs' navigation instruments and charts, were still in place. The ship's food stores were plentiful, with enough provisions to last for months. The lifeboat, however, was missing, suggesting that the crew may have abandoned the ship in it.

One of the most puzzling aspects of the mystery is that the ship appeared to be in good condition. Although some water had entered the ship's hull, it was not enough to threaten the vessel's buoyancy. The sails were set, though some were slightly damaged, and the ship was on a steady course. There was no indication of any catastrophic event that would have forced the crew to abandon the ship so suddenly. In fact, the Mary Celeste seemed capable of continuing her journey, which raises the question of why the crew would have left her in such a hurry.

Theories about the fate of the Mary Celeste's crew began to circulate almost immediately after the ship was found. One of the earliest and most plausible theories was that the crew had feared an explosion due to the volatile nature of the alcohol they were carrying. Denatured alcohol is highly flammable, and it is possible that fumes from the cargo had built up in the ship's hold. If the crew had detected these fumes and feared that an explosion was imminent, they may have hastily abandoned the ship in the lifeboat, intending to return once the danger had passed. However, if this was the case, the crew was never able to return, and no trace of them or the lifeboat was ever found.

Another theory suggests that the crew may have fallen victim to a natural disaster, such as a waterspout or an underwater earthquake, which could have caused panic and led them to abandon the ship. Waterspouts, which are essentially tornadoes over water, are known to be violent and unpredictable. If the Mary Celeste had encountered such a phenomenon, the crew may have believed that the ship was in grave danger and decided to leave it behind. However, this theory also fails to explain why the ship was found largely intact and why there was no sign of the crew after they abandoned it.

Piracy was another theory that gained traction, especially since the Atlantic was known for pirate activity at the time. However, this idea was largely dismissed because the ship's cargo and valuables, including the crew's personal belongings, were undisturbed. Pirates typically looted ships they attacked, and there were no signs of violence or plundering on the Mary Celeste, making it unlikely that the ship had been the victim of a pirate raid.

A more speculative theory involves the possibility of mutiny. Some have suggested that the crew may have rebelled against Captain Briggs, possibly due to tensions aboard the ship or disagreements over how to handle a perceived emergency, such as the potential danger posed by the alcohol cargo. After taking control of the ship, the mutineers could have fled in the lifeboat, though this still doesn't account for the fact that no bodies or wreckage were ever found. Furthermore, Captain Briggs was known to be a fair and competent commander, and his crew was described as trustworthy, making the idea of mutiny less convincing.

There have also been more far-fetched theories, including suggestions that the crew of the Mary Celeste fell prey to paranormal forces or extraterrestrial beings. Some writers and storytellers have speculated that the Bermuda Triangle, a region infamous for mysterious disappearances, could be involved, though the Mary Celeste was actually discovered far outside the area typically associated with the Triangle. Others have even suggested that the crew was abducted by aliens or taken to another dimension, though these ideas are purely in the realm of fiction.

The official investigation into the mystery, conducted by the British Admiralty, concluded that the crew had most likely abandoned ship in a panic, but the exact cause of their decision remains unclear. The lack of any clear evidence, combined with the absence of any survivors or remains, has made it impossible to determine exactly what happened aboard the Mary Celeste. The ship itself, however, continued to sail after being salvaged. It was eventually sold and used in various commercial ventures, but it never fully escaped the shadow of its mysterious past. In 1885, the Mary Celeste was deliberately wrecked off the coast of Haiti as part of an insurance fraud scheme, ending its long and troubled career at sea.

The story of the Mary Celeste has since become the subject of numerous books, articles, and fictional accounts, many of which have embellished or sensationalized the facts of the case. Over time, the mystery has grown into a legend, with each new retelling adding layers of intrigue and speculation. Despite the many theories and investigations, the fate of the crew of the Mary Celeste remains one of the greatest unsolved puzzles in maritime history. The ship's ghostly abandonment, combined with the total disappearance of its crew, has ensured that the mystery of the Mary Celeste will continue to captivate and perplex those who hear the tale.

To this day, the disappearance of the Mary Celeste's crew stands as a symbol of the vast and unpredictable dangers of the open ocean. It reminds us that, despite all of our advances in navigation and communication, the sea holds many secrets, and not all of them are easily explained. Whether the crew succumbed to a tragic accident, fled from a perceived danger, or encountered something even more unusual, their story remains an enduring enigma that will likely never be fully solved. The mystery of the Mary Celeste endures, a haunting chapter in the annals of nautical history, and continues to inspire curiosity and wonder about the many unknowns of the world's oceans.

Chapter 3: The Legend of the USS Cyclops

The legend of the USS *Cyclops* is one of the most enduring and perplexing maritime mysteries associated with the Bermuda Triangle, involving the disappearance of one of the largest fuel ships in the United States Navy during World War I. The *Cyclops*, a massive collier, vanished without a trace in March 1918 while en route from the Caribbean to Baltimore, Maryland. What makes this case so mysterious is that not only did the ship disappear, but none of the 309 crew members and passengers were ever found, nor was any wreckage recovered. This case has given rise to numerous theories, speculation, and legends about what could have happened to the ship, solidifying its place in the lore of the Bermuda Triangle and maritime history.

The USS *Cyclops* was commissioned by the U.S. Navy in 1910 as part of the *Proteus*-class of colliers, vessels designed to carry and transport coal to refuel Navy ships. With a displacement of over 19,000 tons and a length of 540 feet, it was one of the largest and most advanced vessels in the U.S. fleet at the time. The ship was built for long-distance voyages and had powerful engines, though it wasn't particularly fast. Its main function was to serve as a support vessel, providing fuel and supplies to warships stationed around the world. During World War I, when coal-powered ships were essential to maintaining naval operations, the *Cyclops* played a critical role in ensuring that the U.S. Navy remained well-supplied.

On February 16, 1918, the *Cyclops* departed from Rio de Janeiro, Brazil, carrying a heavy load of manganese ore, which was used in the production of steel for the war effort. The ship was under the command of Lieutenant Commander George Worley, a man whose leadership style would later come under scrutiny after the ship's disappearance. The *Cyclops* made a stop in Salvador, Brazil, before heading toward

Barbados in the Caribbean. After departing Barbados on March 4, 1918, the ship was never heard from again. No distress signals were sent, and no one aboard the ship made any attempt to communicate with naval authorities or other ships in the vicinity. The *Cyclops* simply vanished into thin air.

The disappearance of the USS *Cyclops* was especially troubling due to the number of people on board. In addition to the crew of 236 officers and sailors, there were 73 civilian passengers, including engineers, merchants, and workers, many of whom were involved in the war effort. This made the total number of people aboard 309, which was one of the largest losses of life in U.S. Navy history. Despite extensive search efforts, which included ships and aircraft scouring the Atlantic Ocean for weeks, no trace of the *Cyclops* or its passengers was ever found. This lack of evidence or explanation has fueled endless speculation about what could have happened.

One of the most obvious theories is that the USS *Cyclops* was a victim of a catastrophic accident, possibly related to the ship's cargo of manganese ore. Some experts believe that the heavy load of ore may have shifted during the voyage, causing the ship to capsize and sink rapidly. The *Cyclops* was known to be overloaded at the time of its departure, and the extra weight, combined with rough seas, could have led to structural failure or instability. However, this theory doesn't fully explain why no wreckage or debris was ever found, even though ships that sink usually leave behind some trace, such as floating debris, oil slicks, or lifeboats.

Another theory suggests that the USS *Cyclops* may have encountered a powerful storm or rogue wave, which are known to occur in the Atlantic. The Bermuda Triangle, where the *Cyclops* was believed to have disappeared, is infamous for sudden and violent weather patterns, including severe storms and waves that can reach heights of 100 feet or more. If the ship had been caught in such a storm, it could have been overwhelmed and sunk quickly. But again, the lack of any debris or distress signals raises questions about this theory. Even in the case of severe weather, ships usually have enough time to send out a call for help, and remnants of the vessel are often found.

Complicating the mystery further is the fact that Lieutenant Commander George Worley, the captain of the *Cyclops*, had a somewhat controversial reputation. Born in Germany as Johann Frederick Wichmann, Worley immigrated to the United States and changed his name before joining the Navy. Some accounts describe him as a harsh and erratic leader, prone to fits of anger and questionable decision-making. There are unverified reports that the crew was unhappy under his command and that morale aboard the ship was low. This has led to speculation that the ship could have been sabotaged, either by disgruntled crew members or due to some form of mutiny, though no hard evidence supports this theory. Furthermore, the idea of sabotage or mutiny still doesn't explain the complete disappearance of the ship without any trace.

The disappearance of the USS *Cyclops* has also been linked to wartime espionage and enemy action. Some have suggested that the ship may have been sunk by a German submarine or surface raider, as the ship vanished during World War I when German U-boats were patrolling the Atlantic. However, no German records from the time indicate that a U-boat attack on the *Cyclops* occurred, and it's unlikely that the Germans would have kept such a significant attack a secret. Additionally, if the ship had been attacked by a submarine or raider, there would have likely been debris or survivors, as German submarines typically surfaced to attack and allowed crews to abandon ship before sinking vessels. The complete absence of wreckage or survivors makes this theory improbable.

One of the more speculative and far-reaching theories involves the Bermuda Triangle itself. The *Cyclops* disappeared in an area that has become infamous for unexplained phenomena, where ships and planes are said to vanish under mysterious circumstances. Some people believe that the *Cyclops* may have fallen victim to a strange magnetic anomaly or a disturbance in time and space, leading to its sudden disappearance. Others claim that extraterrestrial forces or underwater civilizations could be responsible, abducting the ship and its crew. These ideas, while fascinating, are not supported by any scientific evidence and remain in the realm of fiction and legend.

Over the years, the disappearance of the USS *Cyclops* has spawned numerous books, articles, documentaries, and even fictional stories, each proposing different theories about what happened to the ship and its crew. Despite the wealth of speculation, the true fate of the *Cyclops* remains a mystery. No wreckage has ever been found, and no conclusive evidence has emerged to explain its disappearance. The case is often cited as one of the most baffling in maritime history and is frequently referenced in discussions about the Bermuda Triangle, though the connection to the Triangle itself is largely anecdotal.

Adding to the mystery is the fact that two other ships from the *Proteus* class, the USS *Proteus* and the USS *Nereus*, also disappeared under similar circumstances during World War II while carrying heavy loads of ore. Both ships vanished in the North Atlantic, with no distress signals or wreckage ever found. The loss of these ships, combined with the disappearance of the *Cyclops*, has led some to suggest that there may have been a design flaw in the ships that made them particularly vulnerable when carrying heavy cargo. This theory, while plausible, has never been proven, and the fate of these ships remains as elusive as that of the *Cyclops*.

The legend of the USS *Cyclops* endures not only because of the sheer scale of the tragedy but also because of the complete lack of answers. In an age when modern technology allows for the tracking of ships and planes in real-time, the disappearance of an entire ship with over 300 people aboard without leaving any evidence seems almost unimaginable. The fact that the *Cyclops* was a large, well-known vessel makes the mystery even more perplexing, as ships of that size are usually too significant to simply vanish without a trace.

In recent years, advances in underwater exploration technology, such as sonar mapping and remotely operated vehicles (ROVs), have led to renewed efforts to locate the wreck of the USS *Cyclops*. These technologies have been used to search deep parts of the Atlantic Ocean where the ship is believed to have sunk, but so far, no definitive evidence has been uncovered. The vastness of the ocean, combined with its challenging conditions, makes locating a shipwreck of this nature extremely difficult, and it's possible that the remains of the *Cyclops* may never be found.

The story of the USS *Cyclops* remains one of the most enduring unsolved mysteries of the sea, a reminder of the dangers and unpredictability of ocean travel, even for ships as large and well-equipped as the *Cyclops*. It also serves as a symbol of the unknown forces, both natural and potentially supernatural, that have been attributed to the Bermuda Triangle. Whether the ship was lost to a natural disaster, mechanical failure, or something more mysterious, the disappearance of the USS *Cyclops* continues to capture the imagination of those fascinated by the sea and its many unsolved mysteries. As long as the fate of the ship remains unknown, the legend of the USS *Cyclops* will live on as one of the greatest maritime enigmas of all time.

Chapter 4: The Ghost Ship Ellen Austin

The tale of the *Ellen Austin* is one of the most eerie and fascinating maritime mysteries linked to the Bermuda Triangle, involving a ghost ship that disappeared and reappeared under strange and unexplained circumstances. The *Ellen Austin* was a large American schooner, built in 1854, and was widely known for her role in transporting goods between New York and London. In 1881, during one of her routine transatlantic voyages, the *Ellen Austin* encountered an abandoned vessel in the Sargasso Sea, a region within the Atlantic Ocean notorious for its calm waters, thick seaweed, and puzzling disappearances. The events that followed have since become the stuff of legend, cementing the *Ellen Austin*'s place in the annals of maritime lore.

The story begins in the summer of 1881, when the *Ellen Austin*, under the command of Captain Baker, set sail from London to New York with a cargo of merchandise. The schooner was well-manned, and the voyage across the Atlantic proceeded without incident until the ship reached the area near the Bermuda Triangle. This region, infamous for its mysterious disappearances and strange occurrences, has long been the subject of intrigue and speculation. As the *Ellen Austin* entered the Sargasso Sea, the crew spotted an unidentified vessel adrift in the distance.

Curious and cautious, Captain Baker ordered his crew to approach the ship to investigate. As they drew closer, they observed that the vessel, a large schooner similar to the *Ellen Austin*, appeared to be in good condition, with no signs of damage or distress. However, what struck the crew as particularly odd was the complete absence of any people on board. There were no crew members, no passengers, and no signs of struggle or foul play. The ship was perfectly intact, with its sails set and cargo apparently undisturbed, but it was entirely deserted—a true ghost ship.

The sight of a ship drifting aimlessly across the ocean with no one aboard immediately sparked fear and intrigue among the sailors of the *Ellen Austin*. Ghost ships were not unheard of in maritime history, but their appearance always carried with them a sense of dread and uncertainty. Captain Baker, however, was a pragmatic and experienced seaman. He decided to seize the opportunity, as the abandoned vessel could represent a valuable salvage. After ensuring that the ship was seaworthy, Baker ordered a prize crew of some of his best men to board the ghost ship and sail it alongside the *Ellen Austin* back to New York.

At first, everything seemed to be going according to plan. The two ships sailed in tandem through the calm waters of the Sargasso Sea, with the prize crew now manning the ghost ship. But as the hours passed, the weather took a sudden turn for the worse. A thick fog descended upon the ocean, reducing visibility to almost nothing. The two ships, which had been sailing close together, became separated in the mist. For several hours, the *Ellen Austin* lost sight of the ghost ship, which was now under the control of her prize crew.

When the fog finally lifted, Captain Baker and his crew scanned the horizon, hoping to spot the ghost ship once again. To their relief, the ship eventually reappeared, still intact and seemingly unharmed. However, when the *Ellen Austin* drew closer, Baker and his men were horrified to discover that the ship was once again completely deserted. The prize crew that Baker had sent aboard was gone, just as mysteriously as the original crew. No signs of a struggle, foul play, or accident could be found, and the ship's cargo remained untouched. It was as if the men had simply vanished into thin air.

Baffled but undeterred, Captain Baker made the decision to send another prize crew aboard the ghost ship, determined to salvage it and uncover the truth of what had happened. Once again, the two ships sailed together for several days, but then the strange events repeated themselves. The ghost ship vanished during another period of thick fog, and when it reappeared, the second prize crew had also disappeared, leaving the ship as empty as before. At this point, Baker, thoroughly spooked by the series of inexplicable events, decided to abandon the ghost ship and continue the *Ellen Austin*'s voyage to New York without it.

The ghost ship was never seen again, and no further trace of the men who had been sent aboard it was ever found. The fate of both the original crew and the two prize crews remains one of the great unsolved mysteries of the sea. The disappearance of the men without any signs of violence or disaster has led to endless speculation about what could have happened. Some have suggested that the crew members were abducted, either by pirates, hostile forces, or even supernatural entities, while others believe that they may have fallen victim to a hidden mechanical problem on the ship, such as toxic fumes or gas leaks, which incapacitated and killed them without leaving any visible signs of struggle.

One of the more outlandish theories suggests that the ghost ship may have fallen prey to the Bermuda Triangle's infamous reputation for strange magnetic anomalies, time warps, or other paranormal phenomena. According to this theory, the men may have been swallowed up by some kind of dimensional rift or vortex, causing them to disappear without a trace. This idea, while far-fetched, has been popularized by those who believe that the Bermuda Triangle is a place where the normal laws of physics do not always apply. Others have speculated that the region may have unique magnetic properties that interfere with navigation, communication, and even the perception of reality, leading to strange disappearances and inexplicable phenomena.

The mystery of the *Ellen Austin* and the ghost ship it encountered has also been the subject of numerous fictionalized accounts, many of which embellish or dramatize the facts of the case. Over time, the story has taken on the elements of a classic ghost tale, with each retelling adding new layers of intrigue, suspense, and horror. In some versions of the story, the ghost ship is described as being cursed or haunted, with the spirits of its lost crew still sailing the seas in search of redemption. In others, the ship is said to be a harbinger of doom, appearing to sailors only before disaster strikes. These embellishments, while entertaining, are purely speculative and not supported by historical evidence.

The legend of the *Ellen Austin* and its ghost ship encounter is particularly compelling because of the lack of any concrete explanation. Unlike other maritime mysteries, where shipwrecks, survivors, or wreckage provide some clues as to what may have happened, the *Ellen Austin* case is entirely devoid of such evidence. The men who disappeared left no trace, and the ship itself, which should have been relatively easy to track or identify, was never seen again. This total absence of physical proof has allowed the story to flourish in the realm of legend, where the boundaries between fact and fiction are often blurred.

While the story of the *Ellen Austin* is frequently cited in discussions of the Bermuda Triangle, it's worth noting that the events took place in the Sargasso Sea, which lies to the north of the Triangle's most commonly defined boundaries. The Sargasso Sea has its own reputation for strangeness, largely due to its calm, windless waters, thick mats of seaweed, and frequent reports of ghost ships and derelicts drifting through its expanse. Sailors in the 19th and early 20th centuries often regarded the Sargasso Sea as a place of superstition and fear, where ships could become trapped for weeks or even months in its becalmed waters. The area's peculiar conditions have led to many legends of lost ships and mysterious disappearances, and the *Ellen Austin*'s encounter with the ghost ship is just one of many such tales.

In the decades since the *Ellen Austin*'s ghost ship encounter, maritime historians and researchers have attempted to piece together what might have happened. Some have suggested that the ghost ship was an abandoned vessel that had been left to drift after its crew succumbed to illness, starvation, or exposure. Others believe that the ship may have been the victim of foul play, perhaps attacked by pirates or a rogue crew, who then abandoned the ship when they realized it was of little value. However, none of these theories can account for the disappearance of the prize crews sent aboard by Captain Baker, whose fates remain unknown.

The case of the *Ellen Austin* and its ghost ship remains one of the most enduring mysteries of the sea, a chilling reminder of the dangers and uncertainties that sailors have faced for centuries. The vastness of the ocean, combined with its unpredictable weather and treacherous conditions, has always held the potential for disaster, and the story of the *Ellen Austin* serves as a stark illustration of this. It also underscores the fact that, even in an age of advanced technology and communication, the sea continues to harbor secrets that may never be fully understood or explained.

Today, the legend of the *Ellen Austin* lives on as part of the larger tapestry of maritime folklore. It is a story that has been told and retold countless times, each version adding new details and interpretations, but at its core, the mystery remains unsolved. The ghost ship encountered by the *Ellen Austin* has become a symbol of the unknown, a phantom vessel forever drifting through the fog-shrouded waters of the Atlantic, carrying with it the unanswered questions of what happened to the men who vanished aboard her. Whether the events were the result of natural forces, human error, or something more supernatural, the legend of the *Ellen Austin* will likely continue to captivate and mystify those who hear it for generations to come.

Chapter 5: The Vanishing of the SS Marine Sulphur Queen

The vanishing of the *SS Marine Sulphur Queen* is one of the most perplexing and tragic maritime mysteries in history, particularly within the context of the Bermuda Triangle. The ship, a converted T2 tanker, disappeared in February 1963 while carrying molten sulfur from Beaumont, Texas, to Norfolk, Virginia. Despite extensive search efforts, no trace of the ship or its 39 crew members was ever found, leaving behind only debris and a series of unanswered questions. The *Marine Sulphur Queen*'s disappearance has since become one of the central cases cited in discussions of the Bermuda Triangle and its alleged paranormal activities, though many experts attribute the mystery to more conventional explanations. The story of the *Marine Sulphur Queen* combines elements of engineering failures, dangerous cargo, and unexplained phenomena, making it a compelling narrative that continues to captivate the imagination.

The *SS Marine Sulphur Queen* was originally built during World War II as a T2 tanker, a class of ships designed to transport oil and other petroleum products. The T2 tankers were essential to the war effort, as they provided a steady supply of fuel to Allied forces. After the war, many of these ships were converted for other purposes, including the *Marine Sulphur Queen*, which was modified in 1960 to carry molten sulfur. The ship's cargo tanks were lined with a special heat-resistant material to maintain the sulfur in its molten state, as sulfur needs to be kept at a high temperature to remain liquid. The conversion of the ship was seen as a way to make use of the large number of surplus T2 tankers, which had become less necessary with the end of the war.

However, from the start, there were concerns about the suitability of the *Marine Sulphur Queen* for transporting molten sulfur. The T2 tankers had a reputation for being prone to structural issues, particularly related to their steel hulls, which could become brittle over time. These ships had been designed for short-term use during the war and were not necessarily intended to serve for decades afterward. Additionally, the conversion to a sulfur carrier posed its own set of challenges. Molten sulfur is a highly corrosive and dangerous substance, and the modifications made to the ship did not address all of the potential risks. The ship's new design included a series of large, heated tanks to store the sulfur, but these tanks put significant strain on the ship's structure, particularly in rough seas.

Despite these concerns, the *Marine Sulphur Queen* continued to operate, and on February 2, 1963, the ship departed from Beaumont, Texas, bound for Norfolk, Virginia. The ship was loaded with more than 15,000 tons of molten sulfur, a highly volatile cargo that posed a serious fire risk. The crew of 39 men was led by Captain George T. Worley, an experienced mariner with a long history of commanding ships. The ship set sail under clear skies, and for the first few days of the voyage, there were no reports of trouble.

However, by February 4, 1963, the *Marine Sulphur Queen* had reached the area of the Bermuda Triangle, a region of the Atlantic Ocean notorious for its association with mysterious disappearances of ships and planes. That morning, the ship sent a routine radio message to shore, reporting that all was well and that they were continuing on their course toward Norfolk. This would be the last communication ever received from the *Marine Sulphur Queen*. After that message, the ship vanished without a trace.

When the *Marine Sulphur Queen* failed to arrive in Norfolk as scheduled, a massive search operation was launched by the U.S. Coast Guard. Over the course of several weeks, planes and ships scoured the waters of the Atlantic, particularly focusing on the area where the ship was last known to have been. Despite the extensive efforts, no wreckage of the ship itself was found. However, some small pieces of debris, including life preservers, a life jacket, and parts of the ship's oil tank, were discovered floating in the water. These items were found in the vicinity of the Florida Straits, hundreds of miles from the ship's intended course, suggesting that whatever had happened to the *Marine Sulphur Queen* had occurred in this region.

The discovery of the debris raised more questions than it answered. The fact that the items were found scattered over a wide area suggested that the ship had either broken apart or exploded. However, there was no concrete evidence to determine the exact cause of the ship's disappearance. Some experts speculated that the *Marine Sulphur Queen* may have been destroyed by an explosion caused by its cargo of molten sulfur. Sulfur, when exposed to high temperatures or certain chemical reactions, can become highly flammable and explosive. If a fire had broken out on board, it could have quickly spread to the sulfur tanks, leading to a catastrophic explosion that would have destroyed the ship in seconds. This theory is supported by the fact that no large pieces of the ship were ever found, as would be expected if the ship had exploded.

Another theory suggests that the *Marine Sulphur Queen* may have suffered a structural failure due to the stresses placed on the ship by its cargo and the rough seas of the Atlantic. As a converted T2 tanker, the *Marine Sulphur Queen* was already vulnerable to structural problems, and the addition of the large sulfur tanks likely exacerbated these issues. Some experts believe that the ship may have broken apart at the seams, either due to the weight of the cargo or as a result of the violent motion of the sea. If the ship had broken in two, it would have sunk quickly, leaving little time for the crew to send a distress signal or abandon ship. The scattered debris found in the Florida Straits could be consistent with a ship that had broken apart rather than exploded.

The ship's vanishing also fueled speculation about the involvement of the Bermuda Triangle's alleged paranormal phenomena. The Bermuda Triangle has long been associated with unexplained disappearances, and the loss of the *Marine Sulphur Queen* only added to its mystique. Some theorists believe that the ship may have encountered a strange magnetic anomaly or a powerful undersea disturbance that caused it to vanish without a trace. Others suggest that the Bermuda Triangle is home to otherworldly forces or time warps, which could have swallowed the ship and its crew. These theories, while intriguing, lack any scientific basis, and most experts agree that the disappearance was likely the result of more conventional causes.

The official investigation into the disappearance of the *Marine Sulphur Queen* was conducted by the U.S. Coast Guard, which released its final report in August 1964. The report concluded that the most likely cause of the ship's loss was a combination of structural weaknesses and the dangerous nature of its cargo. The Coast Guard noted that the ship had suffered from significant wear and tear over the years, including cracks in its hull and corrosion in its steel plates. Additionally, the conversion of the ship to carry molten sulfur had placed enormous stress on its structure, making it vulnerable to failure, especially in rough seas. The report also acknowledged the possibility of an explosion, but there was not enough evidence to definitively determine whether a fire or explosion had occurred.

The families of the 39 crew members who perished aboard the *Marine Sulphur Queen* were devastated by the loss and frustrated by the lack of answers. In the years following the ship's disappearance, several lawsuits were filed against the ship's owners, Marine Transport Lines, and the ship's insurers, claiming negligence in the ship's maintenance and operation. The lawsuits alleged that the *Marine Sulphur Queen* was unfit for service and that the company had failed to properly address the known structural issues. While some of these cases were settled out of court, the full truth of what happened to the *Marine Sulphur Queen* may never be known.

The vanishing of the *Marine Sulphur Queen* remains one of the most mysterious shipwrecks in modern history, not only because of the ship's disappearance but also due to the complete lack of conclusive evidence. Unlike other famous shipwrecks, such as the *Titanic* or the *Edmund Fitzgerald*, where the wreckage was eventually located and studied, the *Marine Sulphur Queen* has never been found. The debris recovered from the ship's last known location offers only tantalizing clues, leaving historians, maritime experts, and investigators to speculate about what might have happened.

The case continues to attract attention, particularly among those interested in the mysteries of the Bermuda Triangle. While most experts now believe that the ship's disappearance can be explained by structural failure or an explosion related to its dangerous cargo, the absence of definitive answers leaves room for more fantastic theories to persist. Some even argue that the Bermuda Triangle itself played a role in the ship's vanishing, pointing to the long list of vessels and aircraft that have disappeared in the same region under similarly mysterious circumstances.

Today, the story of the *Marine Sulphur Queen* stands as a sobering reminder of the perils of sea travel, particularly for ships carrying hazardous cargoes. The lessons learned from the ship's disappearance have had a lasting impact on maritime safety regulations, particularly regarding the transport of dangerous materials. The loss of the *Marine Sulphur Queen* also highlights the challenges of investigating maritime disasters, particularly in the vast and often unforgiving environment of the open ocean. Even with modern technology and search techniques, some shipwrecks and disappearances may never be fully explained, leaving behind only questions and speculation.

In the end, the vanishing of the *Marine Sulphur Queen* serves as a testament to the power and unpredictability of the sea, as well as the inherent risks that come with maritime trade and exploration. While the ship's disappearance may never be fully understood, its story will continue to captivate those fascinated by the mysteries of the ocean and the Bermuda Triangle, ensuring that the *Marine Sulphur Queen* remains a part of maritime folklore for generations to come.

Chapter 6: The Bermuda Triangle's Hidden Geography

The Bermuda Triangle's hidden geography is as fascinating as the mysterious disappearances that have made the region notorious. Spanning an area in the western part of the North Atlantic Ocean, the Bermuda Triangle forms a rough triangle with its points at Miami, Florida; Bermuda; and San Juan, Puerto Rico. This region is vast, encompassing around 500,000 to 1.5 million square miles, depending on varying definitions, and it is one of the most heavily traveled shipping lanes in the world. Beneath its surface, however, the Triangle holds a geographical complexity that is often overshadowed by the myths and legends associated with it. The region's hidden geography is defined by its underwater topography, ocean currents, magnetic anomalies, and unique weather patterns, all of which contribute to the area's reputation for strange phenomena. These features combine to create a place where the natural forces of the Earth are both dramatic and, at times, perilous for those traveling above or through its waters.

One of the most striking aspects of the Bermuda Triangle's hidden geography is its diverse underwater terrain. The ocean floor in this region is anything but uniform. It is characterized by sharp drop-offs, deep ocean trenches, and underwater mountain ranges that can dramatically affect both maritime and aerial navigation. Just off the coast of Florida, the continental shelf ends, and the seabed plunges into the deep abyssal plain of the Atlantic Ocean. In some areas, the seafloor drops sharply to depths of more than 12,000 feet. The Puerto Rico Trench, located near the southern boundary of the Bermuda Triangle, is one of the deepest parts of the Atlantic, reaching depths of more than 27,000 feet. This trench is the deepest point in the entire Atlantic Ocean and creates a complex and often unpredictable environment for both oceanographers and mariners.

These deep waters can be treacherous, as they are subject to strong and erratic currents. One of the most significant oceanic features of the Bermuda Triangle is the Gulf Stream, a powerful and fast-moving current that flows from the Gulf of Mexico along the eastern coast of the United States and into the Atlantic. The Gulf Stream is essentially a river within the ocean, moving at speeds of up to 5.6 miles per hour. It can carry debris, vessels, and even entire ships for hundreds of miles before they are discovered—or not. The Gulf Stream is also known for its unpredictable eddies and whirlpools, which can create dangerous conditions for ships and aircraft that stray too close to its path. Sailors have long reported difficulties navigating these waters, as the current can push vessels off course without warning, and sudden shifts in weather patterns are common.

In addition to its deep oceanic features and powerful currents, the Bermuda Triangle's hidden geography includes extensive underwater mountain ranges and volcanic activity. The Mid-Atlantic Ridge, a massive underwater mountain range that runs down the center of the Atlantic Ocean, lies to the east of the Bermuda Triangle. This ridge is part of the global network of mid-ocean ridges where tectonic plates meet and spread apart, leading to volcanic activity and the formation of new oceanic crust. While the Mid-Atlantic Ridge itself does not directly impact the Bermuda Triangle, the tectonic activity in the region contributes to underwater earthquakes, which can trigger tsunamis or sudden shifts in the seafloor.

One of the most interesting geological features in the Bermuda Triangle is the presence of submarine volcanoes and seamounts—underwater mountains formed by volcanic activity. These seamounts rise from the ocean floor, often reaching heights of thousands of feet, yet their peaks remain submerged, creating hazards for ships and submarines. Although not widely known, volcanic activity in the Atlantic Ocean is not uncommon, and underwater eruptions can create massive plumes of gas and steam that rise to the surface. These eruptions can cause sudden and violent changes in the water's surface conditions, potentially contributing to the sudden and mysterious disappearances that the Bermuda Triangle is famous for.

One theory that has been proposed to explain some of the strange phenomena in the Bermuda Triangle involves the release of large amounts of methane gas from the ocean floor. Methane hydrates, which are crystalline structures of water and gas, are found in abundance in certain areas of the ocean floor, particularly in regions of continental margins. When these hydrates destabilize, either due to shifting tectonic plates, underwater landslides, or volcanic activity, they can release vast quantities of methane gas into the water. This gas can rise rapidly to the surface, creating a frothy, bubbling area of water. Some scientists suggest that if a ship were to pass over such a region at the wrong time, the water would lose its buoyancy, causing the ship to sink quickly and without warning. This phenomenon, known as a methane blowout, could explain why some vessels in the Bermuda Triangle seem to disappear without a trace, leaving behind no wreckage or survivors.

Another key feature of the Bermuda Triangle's hidden geography is its complex magnetic environment. The region has long been associated with strange magnetic anomalies, where compasses and other navigational instruments behave erratically. One of the most famous aspects of the Bermuda Triangle lore is the claim that it is one of the few places on Earth where compasses point true north instead of magnetic north. While this was once true, the area where this occurred has since shifted westward due to the natural movement of the Earth's magnetic poles. However, the Bermuda Triangle is still known for its erratic magnetic fields, which can interfere with navigation.

These magnetic anomalies may be caused by variations in the Earth's magnetic field, which are particularly pronounced in regions where tectonic plates meet or where large deposits of iron ore lie beneath the ocean floor. The presence of volcanic activity and shifting tectonic plates in the Bermuda Triangle region could contribute to localized magnetic disturbances. Pilots and sailors have reported instances where their compasses spun wildly or gave false readings, leading them off course and into danger. While these magnetic anomalies are not unique to the Bermuda Triangle, their presence in combination with the region's other geographical hazards makes for a potentially deadly combination.

Weather also plays a significant role in the Bermuda Triangle's hidden geography. The region lies within a zone known as the "Hurricane Alley," where warm waters from the Gulf Stream meet cooler air from the north, creating the perfect conditions for powerful storms. The Bermuda Triangle is frequently hit by hurricanes and tropical storms, particularly during the hurricane season from June to November. These storms can form quickly and with little warning, making them particularly dangerous for ships and aircraft. The sudden and violent nature of these storms has been cited as a possible explanation for some of the disappearances in the Triangle. Hurricanes can produce massive waves, strong winds, and lightning, all of which can destroy ships or cause aircraft to lose control.

In addition to hurricanes, the Bermuda Triangle is also prone to sudden squalls, waterspouts, and microbursts. Squalls are fast-moving storms that can form out of nowhere, bringing heavy rain, strong winds, and rough seas. Waterspouts are tornadoes that form over water, and they can reach speeds of over 100 miles per hour. Microbursts are intense downdrafts of wind that can cause extreme turbulence for aircraft, often leading to crashes. These sudden and unpredictable weather patterns are a significant hazard for anyone traveling through the Bermuda Triangle.

Despite the many natural dangers present in the Bermuda Triangle, the region remains one of the most heavily trafficked in the world, with thousands of ships and aircraft passing through it each year without incident. The majority of these vessels navigate the Triangle's hidden geography without difficulty, thanks to modern navigational technology and weather forecasting. However, the Triangle's reputation for mystery and danger persists, fueled by the occasional disappearance or unexplained event.

While many of the myths surrounding the Bermuda Triangle have been debunked, its hidden geography continues to intrigue scientists and researchers. The region's complex underwater terrain, strong ocean currents, volcanic activity, and unique weather patterns create an environment that is both dynamic and unpredictable. Understanding the natural forces at work in the Bermuda Triangle is key to unraveling the mystery of why so many ships and planes have disappeared in the region.

In recent years, advances in oceanography, geology, and meteorology have shed new light on the Bermuda Triangle's hidden geography. Satellite imaging and deep-sea exploration have revealed more about the underwater landscape, while improved models of ocean currents and weather patterns have helped scientists better understand the region's hazards. These discoveries have provided a more scientific explanation for many of the incidents that have occurred in the Bermuda Triangle, although some mysteries remain unsolved.

One of the most exciting recent developments in the study of the Bermuda Triangle is the use of autonomous underwater vehicles (AUVs) to map the ocean floor in unprecedented detail. These robotic submarines can explore areas of the ocean that were previously inaccessible to humans, providing valuable data on the topography, geology, and biology of the ocean depths. In the Bermuda Triangle, AUVs have been used to study the Puerto Rico Trench and other deep-sea features, helping scientists to better understand the forces shaping the region.

The Bermuda Triangle's hidden geography also holds potential clues to the future of our planet. As scientists study the region's tectonic activity and underwater volcanoes, they are learning more about the processes that shape the Earth's crust and drive the movement of continents. The Triangle's location at the intersection of major ocean currents and weather systems also makes it an important area for climate research. By studying how the Gulf Stream and other currents interact with the atmosphere, scientists can gain insights into how climate change may affect weather patterns and ocean circulation in the future.

In conclusion, the Bermuda Triangle's hidden geography is a complex and multifaceted system of natural forces that contribute to the region's reputation for danger and mystery. The combination of deep ocean trenches, strong currents, underwater volcanoes, magnetic anomalies, and unpredictable weather patterns creates an environment where both human error and natural phenomena can easily lead to disaster. While many of the disappearances in the Bermuda Triangle can be attributed to these natural factors, the region's geography continues to capture the imagination, ensuring that the mystery of the Bermuda Triangle will endure for generations to come.

Chapter 7: The Strange Weather Phenomena

The strange weather phenomena of the Bermuda Triangle have played a significant role in the mystery and intrigue surrounding this area of the Atlantic Ocean. Over the years, sailors, pilots, and scientists have all reported strange and unusual weather events within the Triangle, contributing to the long-standing belief that the region is a place where normal rules of nature don't seem to apply. While many of these phenomena can be explained by science, the sheer intensity and unpredictability of the weather in this part of the world have led to countless stories of disappearances, crashes, and shipwrecks.

The Bermuda Triangle, located between Miami, Bermuda, and Puerto Rico, lies in a region of the Atlantic that is particularly vulnerable to rapid and severe weather changes. This area is part of a larger zone known as "Hurricane Alley," which experiences a high frequency of tropical storms, hurricanes, and other powerful weather systems. The unique geographical and meteorological conditions that converge here make the Bermuda Triangle a hotspot for dramatic and often dangerous weather patterns, some of which have been blamed for the unexplained disappearances of ships and planes in the area.

One of the most significant contributors to the strange weather phenomena in the Bermuda Triangle is its location near the warm waters of the Gulf Stream. The Gulf Stream is a powerful, fast-moving ocean current that originates in the Gulf of Mexico and flows along the eastern coast of the United States before veering out into the Atlantic. As this warm current flows into the cooler waters of the Atlantic Ocean, it can create a range of meteorological effects. For example, the warm, moist air above the Gulf Stream can collide with cooler, drier air from the north, leading to the rapid formation of thunderstorms, squalls, and other severe weather events. These sudden and intense storms can appear with little to no warning, catching sailors and pilots by surprise.

One of the most infamous weather phenomena associated with the Bermuda Triangle is the occurrence of "rogue waves." Rogue waves are enormous, unpredictable waves that can reach heights of up to 100 feet or more. They are often caused by the convergence of multiple smaller waves, which combine to create a massive, towering wall of water. These waves can appear out of nowhere, and their immense size and power make them a serious threat to ships, even large ocean-going vessels. Rogue waves are known to occur in various parts of the world's oceans, but they are particularly dangerous in the Bermuda Triangle due to the region's strong ocean currents and the interaction between the Gulf Stream and the surrounding waters.

The combination of these powerful waves and the fast-moving Gulf Stream can create incredibly hazardous conditions for ships and boats. Vessels caught in the path of a rogue wave may find themselves capsized or overwhelmed by the sheer force of the water. In some cases, ships may sink so quickly that they don't have time to send out a distress signal, contributing to the mysterious disappearances that have been reported in the Bermuda Triangle. While rogue waves are now recognized as a legitimate oceanic phenomenon, their unpredictability and rarity make them difficult to study, and they remain one of the more mysterious elements of the Triangle's strange weather.

Another unusual weather phenomenon that has been reported in the Bermuda Triangle is the appearance of waterspouts. Waterspouts are essentially tornadoes that form over the surface of the ocean, and they can be just as dangerous as their land-based counterparts. Waterspouts typically form during intense thunderstorms, when warm, moist air rises rapidly and begins to rotate, creating a funnel of wind and water that extends from the clouds to the sea below. These spinning columns of air can reach wind speeds of over 100 miles per hour, and they can pose a serious hazard to ships and aircraft that get too close.

Waterspouts are particularly dangerous because they can form quickly and without warning. A ship or plane traveling through seemingly calm waters or skies might suddenly find itself in the path of a violent, twisting waterspout. These spinning storms can easily capsize small boats or disrupt the flight of aircraft, causing mechanical failures or loss of control. Sailors have long reported encounters with waterspouts in the Bermuda Triangle, and some believe that these phenomena may be responsible for the sudden and unexplained disappearances of vessels in the region.

In addition to waterspouts, the Bermuda Triangle is also prone to sudden, violent squalls. Squalls are intense, short-lived storms characterized by heavy rain, strong winds, and sometimes hail or lightning. What makes squalls particularly dangerous is their sudden onset; they can develop in a matter of minutes, leaving little time for sailors or pilots to react. The Bermuda Triangle's position near the Gulf Stream and the warm tropical waters of the Atlantic makes it an ideal breeding ground for these fast-moving storms. Ships or planes that find themselves in the midst of a squall may experience extreme turbulence, rough seas, or mechanical failure, all of which can lead to disaster.

Hurricanes are another major weather phenomenon that impacts the Bermuda Triangle, particularly during the Atlantic hurricane season, which runs from June to November. Hurricanes are massive, rotating storms that can span hundreds of miles and produce sustained winds of over 150 miles per hour. They are fueled by warm ocean waters, and the Bermuda Triangle's location in Hurricane Alley makes it particularly vulnerable to these powerful storms. Hurricanes can produce towering waves, torrential rains, and devastating winds, all of which can wreak havoc on ships and planes traveling through the region.

One of the reasons hurricanes are so dangerous in the Bermuda Triangle is that they can be difficult to predict. While modern meteorology has made great strides in forecasting hurricanes, their exact path and intensity can still be uncertain, especially in the early stages of development. A ship or plane that enters the Bermuda Triangle during hurricane season might find itself caught in the path of a rapidly intensifying storm. The Bermuda Triangle's reputation for strange and sudden disappearances may be partly due to the sheer unpredictability of these massive storms. In the past, before advanced weather forecasting tools were available, many ships and planes may have inadvertently sailed into the path of a hurricane, never to be seen again.

While hurricanes are the most well-known severe weather phenomena in the Bermuda Triangle, smaller but equally dangerous weather events, known as microbursts, can also occur. Microbursts are intense downdrafts of air that can create powerful bursts of wind at the surface, often with speeds exceeding 100 miles per hour. These sudden, violent gusts can be especially dangerous for aircraft, as they can cause severe turbulence or even force planes into the ocean. Microbursts are difficult to detect and predict, making them a particularly dangerous hazard for planes flying over the Bermuda Triangle.

Another curious weather-related phenomenon that has been observed in the Bermuda Triangle is the occurrence of "air bombs" or "hexagonal clouds." These unusual formations were first documented in the early 2000s when satellite imagery revealed large, hexagonal-shaped clouds forming over the Atlantic Ocean, particularly in the Bermuda Triangle region. These clouds are believed to form as a result of powerful microbursts of wind that descend from the atmosphere, hitting the ocean surface with incredible force. The resulting winds, which can reach speeds of up to 170 miles per hour, are strong enough to create massive waves and even sink ships.

The formation of these air bombs or hexagonal clouds is still not fully understood, but some scientists believe that they could be responsible for the sudden and violent weather conditions that have been reported in the Bermuda Triangle. These powerful wind bursts could easily overwhelm ships or planes caught in their path, causing them to disappear without a trace. While the exact relationship between these strange cloud formations and the disappearances in the Bermuda Triangle remains a matter of debate, the discovery of such powerful weather phenomena adds another layer of complexity to the region's already mysterious reputation.

In addition to these well-documented weather phenomena, there are also more speculative and controversial theories about the Bermuda Triangle's strange weather. Some theorists suggest that the region may be home to unusual atmospheric or electromagnetic anomalies that interfere with navigation and communication systems. For example, reports of compasses spinning wildly or giving incorrect readings in the Bermuda Triangle have led to speculation that the area may experience magnetic disturbances. These anomalies could theoretically cause ships and planes to veer off course, leading them into dangerous waters or even causing them to crash or sink.

There are also stories of strange fogs or mists that suddenly envelop ships and planes in the Bermuda Triangle, leading to disorientation and confusion. Pilots have reported flying into a thick, swirling fog, only to emerge miles off course or with their instruments malfunctioning. While these reports are difficult to verify, they have contributed to the sense that the Bermuda Triangle is a place where normal weather patterns and natural laws don't always seem to apply. Some theorists have even suggested that these strange fogs could be linked to time warps or dimensional shifts, though such ideas remain firmly in the realm of science fiction.

Despite the wide range of strange weather phenomena that have been reported in the Bermuda Triangle, it is important to note that many of these events can be explained by natural causes. The region's unique geographical and meteorological conditions make it particularly prone to severe weather, and many of the mysterious disappearances can likely be attributed to these dangerous but ultimately natural phenomena. However, the combination of unpredictable storms, powerful ocean currents, and unusual atmospheric conditions makes the Bermuda Triangle a place where even experienced sailors and pilots can find themselves in trouble.

In recent years, advances in meteorology and satellite technology have helped scientists better understand the weather patterns in the Bermuda Triangle, but many questions still remain. The region's reputation for strange and unexplained disappearances continues to captivate the public's imagination, and the role that weather plays in these mysteries is still a topic of ongoing research. Whether it's rogue waves, waterspouts, hurricanes, or air bombs, the Bermuda Triangle's weather is as unpredictable as it is dangerous, and it will likely continue to be a source of fascination for years to come.

Chapter 8: The Role of Compass Malfunctions

The role of compass malfunctions in the Bermuda Triangle mystery is one of the most intriguing and long-debated aspects of the region's mystique. For centuries, sailors and aviators have reported strange and erratic behavior in their compasses while navigating the Triangle, leading many to believe that the area is subject to powerful and unusual forces that interfere with navigation systems. These compass malfunctions, often seen as one of the contributing factors to the unexplained disappearances of ships and planes in the Bermuda Triangle, have fueled speculation and intrigue for decades.

Compasses are one of the oldest and most reliable tools for navigation, used by sailors and explorers since ancient times to determine direction. They rely on the Earth's magnetic field, which runs from the magnetic North Pole to the magnetic South Pole, allowing a compass needle to align itself with this field and point toward magnetic north. In most places on Earth, this system works predictably and without issue. However, in the Bermuda Triangle, there have been numerous reports of compass malfunctions, with compasses suddenly spinning wildly, pointing in the wrong direction, or simply failing altogether. This has led to many theories about why such malfunctions occur and how they might be linked to the region's reputation for danger and mystery.

One of the most well-known aspects of compass malfunctions in the Bermuda Triangle is the claim that it is one of the few places on Earth where compasses point toward true north instead of magnetic north. Magnetic north, which is the direction a compass needle naturally points, is not exactly the same as true north, which is the geographical North Pole. In most parts of the world, the difference between these two is known as magnetic declination, and navigators must account for it when plotting their course. However, in certain parts of the world, including the Bermuda Triangle, there are reports that compasses may sometimes point directly toward true north without any need for correction. This phenomenon, which has been called the "agonic line," has sparked much speculation and fear among those who navigate the region.

Historically, the Bermuda Triangle was one of the areas where the agonic line, or the point where true north and magnetic north are perfectly aligned, was located. Sailors who were unaware of this could easily have become confused, especially in the days before modern GPS and satellite navigation. A ship's compass pointing toward true north without accounting for magnetic declination could lead to navigational errors, causing vessels to veer off course by hundreds of miles. In an area as vast and unpredictable as the Bermuda Triangle, such errors could prove disastrous, especially if ships sailed into dangerous waters, strong currents, or treacherous weather conditions as a result.

While the agonic line has since shifted westward, moving closer to the Gulf of Mexico and away from the Bermuda Triangle, the region is still notorious for its magnetic anomalies. These anomalies refer to areas where the Earth's magnetic field behaves unpredictably or inconsistently, causing compasses to malfunction. Some theories suggest that these anomalies may be caused by local geological features, such as large deposits of iron ore or underwater volcanic activity, both of which can affect the Earth's magnetic field in localized regions. Others believe that tectonic activity in the area, such as the movement of the Earth's plates, could also contribute to the unusual magnetic behavior observed in the Bermuda Triangle.

One popular theory is that the Bermuda Triangle sits above a particularly volatile section of the Earth's crust, where the movement of tectonic plates or underwater volcanic activity could be generating powerful magnetic fields that interfere with navigation systems. While this is speculative, it is not entirely without scientific basis. The region surrounding the Bermuda Triangle is known for its complex underwater geography, which includes deep ocean trenches, submerged mountain ranges, and volcanic activity. The Puerto Rico Trench, for example, is one of the deepest parts of the Atlantic Ocean and lies close to the southern edge of the Bermuda Triangle. This trench, along with other underwater geological features, could be contributing to the region's magnetic anomalies.

Another possible explanation for the compass malfunctions reported in the Bermuda Triangle is the presence of geomagnetic storms. These storms are caused by solar activity, specifically when charged particles from the sun interact with the Earth's magnetic field. When the sun releases a large burst of energy, known as a solar flare or coronal mass ejection, it can send streams of charged particles toward Earth, disturbing the planet's magnetic field. These disturbances can lead to geomagnetic storms, which have the potential to interfere with navigational systems, including compasses. Geomagnetic storms are known to affect regions near the poles, but they can also impact areas like the Bermuda Triangle, particularly during periods of high solar activity.

During a geomagnetic storm, the Earth's magnetic field can fluctuate wildly, causing compass needles to deviate from their usual alignment. Navigators relying on traditional compass systems may find their readings suddenly inaccurate, leading to confusion and disorientation. This could explain some of the strange compass behavior reported by pilots and sailors in the Bermuda Triangle. In addition, geomagnetic storms can also disrupt radio communications and GPS systems, further complicating navigation in the region. In an area already known for its unpredictable weather and ocean currents, the added challenge of geomagnetic interference could easily result in ships or planes becoming lost or going off course.

The effects of geomagnetic storms are not always immediate or predictable. Sometimes, a storm may cause only minor disruptions, while at other times, the impact can be severe. One of the challenges for navigators in the Bermuda Triangle is that these storms are difficult to predict and may occur without warning. While modern technology has made it easier to monitor solar activity and forecast potential geomagnetic storms, this was not the case in earlier times, when many of the Bermuda Triangle's most famous disappearances occurred. For sailors and pilots in the early 20th century, the sudden onset of a geomagnetic storm could have been catastrophic, especially if it caused their compasses to malfunction at a critical moment.

In addition to geomagnetic storms and geological anomalies, there is also speculation that the Bermuda Triangle may be subject to more exotic and less well-understood forces. Some theorists suggest that the region may experience localized gravitational anomalies or disturbances in the Earth's electromagnetic field, which could interfere with navigation systems in ways that are not yet fully understood. These theories are largely speculative and lack solid scientific evidence, but they have nonetheless contributed to the aura of mystery surrounding the Bermuda Triangle. In popular culture, the idea that the Bermuda Triangle might be a "vortex" or "portal" to another dimension, where the normal rules of physics do not apply, has become a common trope in books, movies, and television shows.

Despite these more fantastical theories, many scientists believe that the compass malfunctions reported in the Bermuda Triangle can be explained by more mundane factors. For example, human error is often cited as a potential cause. In the past, before the advent of modern navigational tools, sailors and pilots relied heavily on compasses and other basic instruments to find their way. However, even a slight error in compass calibration or interpretation could lead to significant navigational mistakes, particularly in a region as vast and open as the Bermuda Triangle. Strong ocean currents, such as the Gulf Stream, could easily push ships off course, while rapidly changing weather conditions could disorient pilots flying over the open ocean.

In some cases, the malfunction of a compass may not be due to any external force at all but rather to mechanical failure. Compasses, like any other piece of equipment, are subject to wear and tear, and a malfunctioning compass could give false readings, leading to navigational errors. This was especially true in the early 20th century when many of the Bermuda Triangle's famous disappearances occurred. Ships and planes of that era were often equipped with relatively simple and less reliable navigational tools compared to the sophisticated systems used today. A single faulty compass could easily lead a ship or plane far off course, particularly in an area as featureless and difficult to navigate as the open ocean.

Another factor that may contribute to compass malfunctions in the Bermuda Triangle is the region's highly variable weather conditions. The Bermuda Triangle is known for its sudden and violent storms, including thunderstorms, squalls, and hurricanes, which can produce strong electrical activity. Lightning strikes, in particular, can have a significant impact on magnetic fields and electrical systems, including compasses. A direct hit from a lightning strike could easily cause a compass to malfunction or give inaccurate readings. Furthermore, the electrical activity associated with thunderstorms can create localized magnetic disturbances, which might temporarily interfere with a ship or plane's navigational instruments.

While many of the compass malfunctions reported in the Bermuda Triangle can be attributed to natural phenomena, mechanical failure, or human error, the sheer number of incidents involving erratic compass behavior in the region continues to fuel speculation and mystery. Over the years, numerous ships and planes have reported problems with their compasses shortly before disappearing, and this has led to the belief that there may be something inherently strange or dangerous about the Bermuda Triangle. Whether these malfunctions are the result of natural forces, human mistakes, or something more mysterious, they remain a key element in the enduring mystery of the Bermuda Triangle.

In modern times, with the advent of advanced satellite navigation systems, GPS, and other technologies, the importance of traditional compasses has diminished. However, compass malfunctions in the Bermuda Triangle continue to be reported, even with modern equipment. This suggests that the region's unique magnetic environment may still be playing a role in navigation difficulties. While many of the disappearances in the Bermuda Triangle may be explained by other factors, the possibility of compass malfunctions remains an important part of the puzzle, and it continues to be a subject of scientific inquiry and debate.

In conclusion, the role of compass malfunctions in the Bermuda Triangle mystery is multifaceted, with possible explanations ranging from natural magnetic anomalies and geomagnetic storms to human error and mechanical failure. While many of these phenomena can be explained by science, the unpredictable and often erratic behavior of compasses in the region has contributed significantly to the Triangle's reputation as a dangerous and mysterious place. Whether caused by the unique geography of the area, powerful magnetic forces, or simply the fallibility of human navigation, compass malfunctions will likely remain a key aspect of the Bermuda Triangle's enduring legend.

Chapter 9: Theories of Alien Abductions

Theories of alien abductions in connection to the Bermuda Triangle have captured the imaginations of both believers in extraterrestrial life and conspiracy theorists for decades. The unexplained disappearances of ships, planes, and people in this vast stretch of the Atlantic Ocean have given rise to countless speculative explanations, and one of the most sensational and enduring is the idea that aliens are responsible. According to this theory, the Bermuda Triangle is not just a region of dangerous weather patterns or natural magnetic anomalies, but a hotbed of extraterrestrial activity where aliens abduct humans and vessels for unknown purposes.

The connection between the Bermuda Triangle and aliens first gained widespread attention in the mid-20th century, particularly during the 1940s and 1950s, when interest in UFOs and extraterrestrial life was booming in popular culture. In the aftermath of World War II, technological advances, particularly in aviation, led to an increase in the number of aircraft flying over the Bermuda Triangle, and several high-profile disappearances during this period sparked renewed interest in the mystery of the Triangle. One of the most famous incidents was the disappearance of Flight 19, a group of U.S. Navy bombers that vanished without a trace during a routine training mission in 1945. The aircraft and their crews were never found, and this fueled speculation that something beyond the realm of normal human experience might be at work in the region.

Theories about alien involvement in the Bermuda Triangle often draw on the idea that extraterrestrials are using the area as a base or portal for their activities. Proponents of this theory suggest that the Triangle might be home to an underwater alien base or a hidden portal to another dimension, where ships and planes are taken as part of a larger extraterrestrial agenda. According to this line of thinking, the mysterious disappearances in the Bermuda Triangle are not accidents or natural phenomena, but deliberate actions carried out by intelligent beings from another world.

One of the central ideas behind the alien abduction theory is the concept of UFOs, or unidentified flying objects, being sighted in the Bermuda Triangle region. Reports of strange lights in the sky, unexplained aerial phenomena, and unidentified flying objects have been a recurring theme in the accounts of sailors, pilots, and others who have traveled through the Triangle. These sightings are often described as involving bright lights, unusual movements, or aircraft-like objects that do not conform to any known human technology. Some witnesses have even reported seeing strange, disc-shaped craft hovering over the water or moving at incredible speeds before vanishing.

The idea that these UFO sightings are linked to alien abductions stems from the belief that extraterrestrials are monitoring or experimenting with human beings. Some theories suggest that the disappearances in the Bermuda Triangle are the result of alien experiments, with humans and their vessels being taken aboard UFOs for study. In this scenario, the people and objects that vanish in the Triangle are not simply lost at sea, but are being transported to other locations—either on Earth or in space—for unknown purposes. This idea has been popularized in many works of science fiction, which often depict the Bermuda Triangle as a sort of "alien hunting ground" where extraterrestrials capture human subjects for experimentation.

Supporters of the alien abduction theory often point to the fact that many of the disappearances in the Bermuda Triangle have occurred without leaving any physical evidence behind. Ships have vanished without a single piece of wreckage washing ashore, and planes have disappeared from radar without any distress signals being sent. This has led some to speculate that the technology used by the supposed extraterrestrials is so advanced that it can transport entire vessels and their crews instantaneously, leaving no trace of their presence. In this view, the sudden and unexplained nature of the disappearances in the Triangle is best explained by the involvement of an advanced, non-human intelligence with capabilities far beyond our own.

Another element of the alien abduction theory is the idea that the Bermuda Triangle may serve as a kind of interdimensional gateway or portal. Some theorists propose that the Triangle is located at a point on Earth where the boundaries between dimensions or realities are thinner than elsewhere, allowing extraterrestrial beings to travel between their world and ours. This concept, often referred to as a "vortex" or "wormhole" theory, suggests that the disappearances in the Bermuda Triangle are the result of ships and planes being pulled into another dimension or parallel universe. According to this line of thinking, aliens might be using the Bermuda Triangle as a point of entry or exit from our world, and the people who vanish there are not lost at sea, but are instead transported to another realm entirely.

One of the most famous proponents of the alien abduction theory was Charles Berlitz, an American author who popularized the Bermuda Triangle mystery in the 1970s. Berlitz wrote several books on the subject, including *The Bermuda Triangle*, in which he speculated that extraterrestrial forces could be responsible for the region's many disappearances. Berlitz's work was influential in spreading the idea that aliens might be involved in the Triangle's mysteries, and his books helped cement the region's place in popular culture as a hotspot for paranormal and extraterrestrial activity.

Berlitz's theories were not without their critics, however. Skeptics argue that there is no concrete evidence to support the idea of alien involvement in the Bermuda Triangle, and that many of the disappearances can be explained by natural phenomena, human error, or accidents. For example, ships and planes that disappear in the region may be the victims of severe weather, strong ocean currents, or mechanical failure. In these cases, wreckage may simply be carried away by the Gulf Stream or lost in the depths of the ocean, making it difficult to recover. Furthermore, advances in technology, such as GPS and satellite tracking, have greatly reduced the number of unexplained disappearances in the Bermuda Triangle in recent decades, leading many to believe that the region's reputation is based more on legend than on fact.

Despite these objections, the alien abduction theory continues to have a strong following among those who believe in UFOs and extraterrestrial life. For many, the idea that the Bermuda Triangle is a center of alien activity offers an exciting and otherworldly explanation for the region's mysteries. Some researchers have even gone so far as to suggest that the Bermuda Triangle is part of a larger global network of "alien hotspots" where extraterrestrials are believed to be active. This network includes other mysterious locations such as the Nazca Lines in Peru, the Pyramids of Egypt, and Stonehenge in England—all of which are believed by some to be connected to alien visitations.

One of the more outlandish variations of the alien abduction theory involves the idea that the Bermuda Triangle is linked to the lost city of Atlantis, a legendary advanced civilization that some believe was destroyed by a cataclysmic event. According to this theory, Atlantis may have been an ancient alien colony, and the remnants of its technology—possibly including advanced energy sources or teleportation devices—are still active beneath the waters of the Bermuda Triangle. In this scenario, the strange magnetic anomalies, compass malfunctions, and disappearances reported in the region are the result of alien technology left over from Atlantis, which continues to operate in the present day. This theory blends elements of ancient astronaut speculation with the Bermuda Triangle mystery, creating a rich and complex narrative of alien involvement that spans thousands of years.

While the alien abduction theory remains highly speculative, it has captured the public's imagination in a way that few other explanations for the Bermuda Triangle have. The idea that extraterrestrials might be responsible for the region's mysteries taps into humanity's fascination with the unknown and our ongoing quest to understand our place in the universe. Whether or not aliens are actually involved in the disappearances of ships and planes in the Bermuda Triangle, the theory has become an integral part of the region's mythology, and it continues to be a popular subject for books, movies, and television shows.

In addition to its role in popular culture, the alien abduction theory has also influenced the study of ufology, or the investigation of UFOs and extraterrestrial phenomena. Ufologists have long considered the Bermuda Triangle to be one of the most significant locations on Earth for UFO activity, and many believe that further investigation into the region could yield important insights into the nature of alien visitations. Some ufologists have even conducted expeditions to the Bermuda Triangle in an attempt to capture evidence of UFOs or extraterrestrial life, though these efforts have yet to produce any definitive proof.

The alien abduction theory also intersects with broader ideas about government conspiracies and cover-ups. Some conspiracy theorists believe that governments around the world, particularly the United States, are aware of the extraterrestrial activity in the Bermuda Triangle but are actively concealing the truth from the public. According to this theory, the disappearances in the Bermuda Triangle are part of a larger global pattern of alien abductions that are being hidden from the public to prevent panic or to maintain control over extraterrestrial technology. This idea has been fueled by documents released under the Freedom of Information Act, which reveal that the U.S. government has conducted investigations into UFO sightings and unexplained phenomena, though these investigations have not provided any concrete evidence of alien involvement in the Bermuda Triangle.

In conclusion, the theory of alien abductions in the Bermuda Triangle is a fascinating and highly speculative explanation for the region's many mysteries. While there is no solid scientific evidence to support the idea that extraterrestrials are responsible for the disappearances of ships and planes, the theory has nonetheless become a key part of the Bermuda Triangle's enduring allure. Whether seen as a serious hypothesis or as a work of science fiction, the idea of aliens abducting humans from the Bermuda Triangle continues to captivate imaginations and fuel debate. As long as the Bermuda Triangle remains a place of intrigue and mystery, the theory of alien abductions will likely endure as one of the most compelling and provocative explanations for the unexplained events that have occurred there.

Chapter 10: The Myth of the Atlantis Connection

The myth of the Atlantis connection to the Bermuda Triangle is one of the most captivating and enduring stories surrounding this mysterious region. Atlantis, the legendary island first described by the ancient Greek philosopher Plato, is said to have been an advanced civilization that sank beneath the ocean in a single day and night of misfortune. Over the centuries, the idea of Atlantis has captured the imaginations of scholars, explorers, and conspiracy theorists alike, with many searching for the lost city in various locations around the world. One of the most intriguing theories that has emerged is the belief that Atlantis lies beneath the waters of the Bermuda Triangle, its ancient technology continuing to influence the strange phenomena reported in the region.

The story of Atlantis comes from two of Plato's dialogues, *Timaeus* and *Critias*, written around 360 BCE. According to Plato, Atlantis was a vast island located "beyond the Pillars of Hercules" (what we now call the Strait of Gibraltar), and it was home to an advanced civilization that possessed great wealth, technology, and knowledge. However, due to the Atlanteans' moral decline and their attempt to conquer other lands, they incurred the wrath of the gods. As punishment, the entire island was swallowed by the sea in a catastrophic event. For centuries, scholars have debated whether Atlantis was a real place or simply a moral allegory created by Plato to illustrate the dangers of hubris and imperialism. Despite the lack of definitive evidence for the existence of Atlantis, many have speculated that the story may have been based on real historical events, such as the destruction of ancient civilizations by natural disasters like volcanic eruptions or tsunamis.

The link between Atlantis and the Bermuda Triangle did not gain widespread attention until the 20th century, when the mystery of the Triangle itself became a popular topic of discussion. The idea that

Atlantis might be connected to the strange disappearances in the Bermuda Triangle was first popularized in the 1960s and 1970s, when the Triangle began to gain notoriety as a region where ships and planes vanished without a trace. Some writers and theorists proposed that Atlantis, rather than being located in the Mediterranean or elsewhere, was actually submerged somewhere in the Atlantic Ocean, possibly in the area now known as the Bermuda Triangle. This theory suggests that the remnants of Atlantean technology are still active beneath the ocean, causing the magnetic anomalies, compass malfunctions, and disappearances that have come to define the mystery of the Bermuda Triangle.

One of the key elements of the Atlantis-Bermuda Triangle connection is the idea that the ancient Atlanteans possessed advanced technology that was far beyond anything known in the modern world. According to this theory, the Atlanteans may have developed technologies that could manipulate energy, control the weather, or even distort space and time. Some proponents of the Atlantis connection believe that these technologies were so powerful that they continue to function even after the island sank beneath the sea, creating the strange and dangerous conditions that make the Bermuda Triangle so notorious. For example, the theory suggests that Atlantean energy devices, possibly powered by crystals or some other unknown source, could be responsible for the disruptions in navigation equipment, such as the compass malfunctions reported by sailors and pilots in the Triangle.

Crystals, in particular, play a prominent role in many Atlantis theories. Some writers suggest that the Atlanteans harnessed the power of giant crystals as a source of energy, using them for everything from communication to transportation. These crystals, it is argued, may still exist on the ocean floor, and their energy could be interfering with the magnetic field in the Bermuda Triangle, causing the strange phenomena reported there. The idea of energy-emitting crystals is often tied to the concept of "ley lines" or "energy grids," which are believed by some to be invisible lines of power that crisscross the Earth. According to this theory, Atlantis was located at a key point on this energy grid, and the Bermuda Triangle may be another such point where the energy is especially strong or unstable.

One of the most famous proponents of the Atlantis-Bermuda Triangle connection was Charles Berlitz, an American author who wrote extensively about the mysteries of the Triangle. In his 1974 book *The Bermuda Triangle*, Berlitz speculated that the lost city of Atlantis might lie at the bottom of the Triangle and that its advanced technology could explain the strange occurrences in the area. Berlitz's work was influential in popularizing the idea that Atlantis and the Bermuda Triangle were linked, and his books helped bring the mystery of the Triangle to a global audience. While Berlitz's theories were widely criticized by mainstream scholars and scientists, they struck a chord with readers and contributed to the ongoing fascination with both Atlantis and the Bermuda Triangle.

The Atlantis-Bermuda Triangle connection has been further fueled by reports of unusual underwater structures found in the region. In the late 1960s and early 1970s, a series of underwater rock formations were discovered off the coast of Bimini, an island in the Bahamas that lies within the boundaries of the Bermuda Triangle. These formations, now known as the Bimini Road, consist of large, flat stones that appear to be arranged in a straight line, leading some to believe that they are the remnants of an ancient man-made structure, possibly part of Atlantis. The discovery of the Bimini Road sparked intense speculation that it could be evidence of the lost city, though many scientists believe that the formations are natural rather than the work of human hands.

Despite the skepticism of the scientific community, the discovery of the Bimini Road has become a central piece of evidence for those who believe in the Atlantis-Bermuda Triangle connection. Some theorists suggest that the road may have been part of a larger complex of Atlantean structures that are now buried beneath the ocean floor. Others propose that the road could be linked to the advanced transportation systems of the Atlanteans, perhaps serving as a landing strip or a pathway for vehicles powered by crystal energy. The idea that Atlantis could have been located in the Caribbean or Atlantic regions has led to further exploration of underwater ruins and formations in the area, with some researchers continuing to search for physical evidence of the lost city.

The connection between Atlantis and the Bermuda Triangle is also supported by the theory that the disappearance of Atlantis itself was related to a natural disaster, such as a massive earthquake, tsunami, or volcanic eruption. Proponents of this idea suggest that the same geological forces that destroyed Atlantis may still be active in the Bermuda Triangle, creating dangerous conditions for ships and planes. For example, some researchers have proposed that the Bermuda Triangle is located near a tectonic plate boundary or an area of intense volcanic activity, where sudden underwater earthquakes or eruptions could cause ships to sink or planes to crash. The idea that the region is prone to natural disasters ties into the broader mythology of Atlantis as a civilization destroyed by a cataclysmic event, and it offers a possible explanation for why so many vessels have vanished in the Triangle.

In addition to the geological theories, there are more speculative and mystical ideas about the Atlantis-Bermuda Triangle connection. Some proponents believe that Atlantis was not just an advanced civilization but a spiritually enlightened society that possessed knowledge of the cosmos, the nature of reality, and the forces of the universe. According to this view, the Atlanteans may have developed technologies that allowed them to manipulate the fabric of space and time, and these technologies may still be active beneath the Bermuda Triangle. This theory suggests that the disappearances in the Triangle are not the result of accidents but are caused by shifts in space-time created by Atlantean devices, which could be responsible for transporting ships and planes to other dimensions or realities.

The idea that Atlantis was connected to higher spiritual or cosmic forces is often linked to the New Age movement, which has embraced the myth of Atlantis as a symbol of a lost golden age of enlightenment and harmony with nature. In this context, the Bermuda Triangle is seen as a place where the energies of Atlantis are still present and where individuals may experience heightened consciousness, psychic phenomena, or even contact with extraterrestrial beings. This mystical interpretation of the Atlantis-Bermuda Triangle connection suggests that the region is not just dangerous but is also a portal to higher realms of existence, where the legacy of Atlantis continues to influence the world.

While the theory of an Atlantis connection to the Bermuda Triangle is popular in certain circles, it has been met with considerable skepticism from the scientific community. Most mainstream historians and archaeologists reject the idea that Atlantis ever existed, viewing Plato's account as a fictional allegory rather than a historical record. Likewise, geologists and oceanographers point out that there is no credible evidence to support the idea that a large, advanced civilization once existed in the area now known as the Bermuda Triangle. The natural explanations for the region's disappearances—such as strong ocean currents, unpredictable weather, and human error—are seen by most experts as more plausible than the idea of ancient technology or mystical forces at work.

Despite these criticisms, the myth of the Atlantis connection to the Bermuda Triangle continues to thrive, thanks in large part to its appeal as a fantastical and romantic explanation for the mysteries of the region. The story of Atlantis, with its themes of a lost golden age, advanced technology, and divine punishment, resonates with the human desire to explore the unknown and to uncover hidden truths about our past. The idea that a civilization as great as Atlantis could have existed and then vanished without a trace is both thrilling and tragic, and it speaks to our fascination with the possibility that there are still secrets waiting to be discovered beneath the ocean's depths.

In popular culture, the Atlantis-Bermuda Triangle connection has been explored in numerous books, films, and television shows. The idea of a sunken city with advanced technology that continues to influence the world today is a staple of science fiction and adventure stories. Movies like *Journey to the Center of the Earth* and TV shows like *Stargate Atlantis* have drawn on the myth of Atlantis to create thrilling narratives about lost civilizations and hidden technologies. The Bermuda Triangle, with its aura of danger and mystery, provides the perfect backdrop for these stories, adding an extra layer of intrigue to the legend of Atlantis.

In conclusion, the myth of the Atlantis connection to the Bermuda Triangle is a captivating and multifaceted theory that combines elements of ancient history, advanced technology, and mystical speculation. Whether seen as a serious hypothesis or a fanciful tale, the idea that Atlantis lies beneath the Bermuda Triangle continues to fuel imaginations and inspire exploration. While there is no scientific evidence to support the theory, its enduring appeal lies in its ability to evoke the wonder and mystery of the unknown. As long as the Bermuda Triangle remains an enigmatic and dangerous place, the legend of Atlantis will continue to be intertwined with its story, offering a tantalizing glimpse into the possibility that the secrets of an ancient civilization may still lie hidden beneath the waves.

Chapter 11: The Bermuda Triangle in Pop Culture

The Bermuda Triangle has been a source of fascination and mystery for decades, capturing the imagination of people worldwide and becoming a rich subject in popular culture. Over time, it has evolved into a symbol of the unknown, inspiring countless works of literature, films, television shows, music, and other media. Its enigmatic nature, along with the mysterious disappearances of ships, planes, and people, has made it an ideal backdrop for storytelling, speculation, and adventure, leading to its inclusion in pop culture in many forms. The mystery of the Bermuda Triangle is not just about the disappearances themselves but also about humanity's endless curiosity about the unknown and our desire to explore the limits of what we understand about the world.

One of the earliest works that popularized the Bermuda Triangle was a book by Charles Berlitz, titled *The Bermuda Triangle*, published in 1974. This book played a key role in introducing the concept to a wide audience. Berlitz, an American author known for writing about paranormal phenomena, compiled various cases of disappearances in the Triangle and presented them as unexplained events, suggesting possible supernatural or extraterrestrial causes. His book became a bestseller, solidifying the Bermuda Triangle's status as a cultural icon of mystery. While Berlitz's work was criticized by skeptics and scientists for its lack of evidence and for stretching the facts, it undeniably fueled the public's interest in the Triangle and cemented its place in popular culture.

Following the publication of Berlitz's book, the Bermuda Triangle became the subject of a wave of films, television specials, and documentaries. In 1975, the documentary film *The Devil's Triangle* was released, further spreading the mystique of the area. The film explored various incidents and theories related to the Triangle, including the possibility of alien abductions, time warps, and underwater cities like Atlantis. The success of the film, combined with the rising interest in paranormal phenomena during the 1970s, helped to perpetuate the idea that the Bermuda Triangle was a place where the normal rules of nature did not apply.

As the fascination with the Bermuda Triangle grew, it became a frequent theme in science fiction and adventure genres, often portrayed as a gateway to other dimensions or as a site for extraterrestrial activity. The idea that the Bermuda Triangle might be a portal to another world has been explored in numerous works of fiction, from novels to comic books to television shows. The notion of strange forces at work in the Triangle allows for endless creative possibilities, making it a fertile ground for writers and filmmakers to explore supernatural and fantastical elements.

In television, the Bermuda Triangle has been featured in both fictional series and documentary-style programs. One of the earliest television shows to explore the Triangle was *In Search of...*, a series hosted by Leonard Nimoy that aired in the 1970s. The show focused on investigating unexplained phenomena, and the Bermuda Triangle was one of its most popular topics. The episode devoted to the Triangle combined dramatic reenactments with expert interviews and speculation, fueling public interest in the region. Other TV shows, such as *The Twilight Zone*, *The X-Files*, and *Unsolved Mysteries*, have also incorporated the Bermuda Triangle into their episodes, often using it as a setting for paranormal or extraterrestrial events.

The science fiction series *The Time Tunnel*, which aired in the 1960s, offered a particularly memorable take on the Bermuda Triangle, imagining it as a place where the laws of time and space could be manipulated. The episode titled "The Ghost of Nero" depicted a ship trapped in the Bermuda Triangle, where characters found themselves moving through time in strange and unpredictable ways. This concept of time distortion in the Triangle has been a recurring theme in many subsequent works of fiction, contributing to the idea that the region is not just dangerous but also a place where the boundaries between different dimensions or realities are blurred.

The Bermuda Triangle has also been a prominent theme in film. The 1978 movie *The Bermuda Triangle*, directed by René Cardona Jr., was one of the first major feature films to focus on the mystery. In the film, a family sailing in the region encounters supernatural phenomena, including ghostly apparitions and mysterious disappearances. While not critically acclaimed, the movie introduced many viewers to the concept of the Bermuda Triangle and helped to cement its reputation as a dangerous and eerie location. Over the years, various other films have followed suit, using the Triangle as a setting for horror, adventure, and thriller stories. Examples include *The Triangle* (2001), a made-for-TV movie about a group of friends who venture into the Triangle in search of a missing ship, and *Triangle* (2009), a psychological horror film that incorporates themes of time loops and alternate realities.

In addition to fiction, documentaries about the Bermuda Triangle continue to captivate audiences. National Geographic, the History Channel, and the Discovery Channel have all produced specials dedicated to the region, exploring both the mystery and the science behind the disappearances. These programs often feature interviews with experts in fields such as oceanography, meteorology, and aviation, offering possible explanations for the strange phenomena while keeping the allure of the mystery alive. The combination of scientific investigation and the region's eerie reputation ensures that these documentaries remain popular, even among viewers who may not believe in supernatural explanations.

The Bermuda Triangle has also left its mark on literature, particularly in the genres of science fiction, adventure, and fantasy. In addition to Charles Berlitz's *The Bermuda Triangle*, numerous other authors have written about the region, either as the central theme of their books or as a setting for larger narratives. Clive Cussler, a popular adventure novelist, has featured the Bermuda Triangle in several of his works. In his novel *Atlantis Found* (1999), the protagonist encounters a mysterious underwater city in the Triangle, tying together the myths of Atlantis and the Bermuda Triangle in a high-stakes adventure. Other authors, such as Graham Hancock and David Childress, have written non-fiction books exploring the possibility that ancient civilizations or extraterrestrial forces might be behind the disappearances in the Triangle.

The mystery of the Bermuda Triangle has also found its way into children's literature and young adult fiction. Many adventure stories aimed at younger readers use the Triangle as a thrilling setting for action-packed quests and explorations. For example, the book *The 39 Clues: Vespers Rising* by Rick Riordan, Gordon Korman, and others features a chase through the Bermuda Triangle, where the characters encounter strange occurrences and hidden dangers. These stories often blend elements of fantasy, mystery, and science fiction, encouraging young readers to explore their curiosity about the world's unexplained phenomena while enjoying the thrill of adventure.

In the realm of music, the Bermuda Triangle has also made its mark, often as a symbol of danger, mystery, or the unknown. In the 1981 song "Bermuda Triangle" by Barry Manilow, the singer describes the Triangle as a place where love disappears without warning, using the region's mysterious reputation as a metaphor for romantic loss. Other songs, such as Fleetwood Mac's "Bermuda Triangle" (1974), use the region as a metaphor for personal or emotional turmoil, suggesting that the uncertainties and dangers of the Triangle mirror the unpredictability of life itself.

Video games have also explored the Bermuda Triangle as a setting for action, mystery, and exploration. In the 2003 game *Crimson Skies: High Road to Revenge*, players fly through a fictionalized version of the Bermuda Triangle, where they encounter sky pirates and mysterious phenomena. The Triangle's aura of danger and adventure makes it a perfect backdrop for video games that emphasize exploration, combat, and the unknown. In the 2013 game *Tomb Raider*, the Bermuda Triangle is suggested as one of the locations that the protagonist, Lara Croft, may have encountered on her adventures, further contributing to its reputation as a place of peril and mystery in the gaming world.

The enduring appeal of the Bermuda Triangle in pop culture can also be attributed to its flexibility as a symbol. It can represent danger, the unknown, otherworldly forces, or even the power of nature. The fact that it has no fixed or definitive explanation allows writers, filmmakers, and artists to interpret it in countless ways. Whether as a literal danger zone where ships and planes vanish without a trace, or as a metaphor for human fear of the unknown, the Bermuda Triangle's ambiguity and mystery have made it an ideal subject for artistic expression and speculative storytelling.

In the realm of conspiracy theories, the Bermuda Triangle holds a prominent place, often linked to extraterrestrials, secret government experiments, or even time travel. These theories have taken root not just in popular media but also in the collective imagination, with people across the world intrigued by the idea that the region might hold secrets beyond our understanding. Conspiracy theorists have proposed that the Triangle could be home to alien bases, that it is a portal to another dimension, or that the U.S. government is covering up knowledge of advanced technology hidden in the area. These ideas have been explored in countless books, documentaries, and online forums, feeding into the ongoing allure of the Bermuda Triangle as a source of endless speculation.

In conclusion, the Bermuda Triangle's role in popular culture is vast and varied, touching nearly every form of media, from books and films to television, music, and video games. Its mysterious reputation and the lack of a definitive explanation for the strange occurrences in the region have made it a symbol of the unknown, a canvas upon which storytellers can project their wildest imaginings. Whether viewed as a literal place of danger or a metaphor for humanity's fear of the unexplained, the Bermuda Triangle continues to captivate audiences and inspire creativity. Its place in popular culture shows no signs of fading, as the mystery and intrigue surrounding the region remain as compelling as ever.

Chapter 12: The Unsolved Case of Star Tiger and Star Ariel

The unsolved case of the *Star Tiger* and *Star Ariel* is one of the most puzzling mysteries associated with the Bermuda Triangle, adding to the legend of this enigmatic region. Both planes were part of the British South American Airways (BSAA) fleet, and their disappearances within a year of each other, under eerily similar circumstances, have baffled investigators for decades. These two events stand as prime examples of how the Bermuda Triangle earned its reputation as a zone where aircraft and ships vanish without a trace, leaving behind more questions than answers.

The first incident involved the *Star Tiger*, a British Avro Tudor IV airliner, which disappeared on January 30, 1948. The aircraft was en route from Santa Maria in the Azores to Bermuda, carrying 25 passengers and six crew members. Captain B.W. McMillan, an experienced pilot, was in command of the flight, and despite some initial concerns about weather conditions, the crew proceeded with the journey. The flight plan involved flying at a low altitude, below 2,000 feet, in order to avoid strong headwinds at higher altitudes, a common practice at the time to conserve fuel.

The journey began normally, and for much of the flight, everything seemed to be going smoothly. However, communication between the *Star Tiger* and ground stations gradually became sparse as the aircraft neared Bermuda. At 3:15 a.m., the last radio transmission from the *Star Tiger* was received, stating that the plane was approximately 380 miles away from Bermuda and that all was well. There were no distress signals or reports of mechanical trouble. After this, the *Star Tiger* simply vanished. When the plane failed to arrive at its scheduled time, an extensive search and rescue operation was launched, involving planes and ships from the U.S. Navy, the British Royal Air Force, and the U.S. Coast Guard. Despite combing the waters and skies for days, no trace of the aircraft, its passengers, or any wreckage was ever found.

The disappearance of the *Star Tiger* immediately attracted widespread attention. Given the fact that the weather conditions, while not ideal, were not considered severe enough to cause such a catastrophic event, speculation ran wild. Many wondered how a large airliner could simply vanish without leaving any debris or clues behind. Some speculated that the aircraft might have been brought down by mechanical failure, possibly due to fuel exhaustion or engine trouble, though no concrete evidence was ever found to support these theories. The *Star Tiger*'s vanishing in the Bermuda Triangle reinforced the growing belief that the region harbored some inexplicable danger, with theories ranging from magnetic anomalies to more fantastical ideas involving supernatural forces.

As if the disappearance of the *Star Tiger* wasn't mysterious enough, the case took an even stranger turn less than a year later with the loss of another BSAA aircraft, the *Star Ariel*. On January 17, 1949, just shy of the first anniversary of the *Star Tiger*'s disappearance, the *Star Ariel* departed from Bermuda, bound for Kingston, Jamaica. The *Star Ariel* was another Avro Tudor IV airliner, nearly identical to the *Star Tiger*, and was commanded by Captain John Clutha McPhee. Like McMillan, McPhee was an experienced and respected pilot, and there was no indication that the flight would encounter any significant difficulties. The weather on that day was reported to be clear and calm, with excellent visibility.

The *Star Ariel* took off at 8:41 a.m., and soon after departure, Captain McPhee contacted Bermuda's ground control to report that the aircraft had climbed to 18,000 feet and was cruising smoothly. At 9:42 a.m., McPhee radioed again to provide his position, confirming that everything was normal and that the flight was proceeding as planned. It was the last communication ever received from the aircraft.

Much like the *Star Tiger*, the *Star Ariel* vanished without a trace, leaving no evidence of what might have happened.

Once again, a massive search and rescue operation was initiated, but it yielded no results. No wreckage, oil slicks, or bodies were found, and the aircraft's disappearance became another Bermuda Triangle mystery. The similarities between the two cases were striking: both involved Avro Tudor IV airliners from the same airline, both flights took place in or around the Bermuda Triangle, and in both cases, the planes vanished suddenly, without any distress signals or known technical issues. These coincidences only deepened the mystery and fueled speculation that something unusual was happening in the region.

One of the major challenges in understanding what happened to both the *Star Tiger* and the *Star Ariel* is the complete lack of physical evidence. In aviation accidents, investigators often rely on wreckage, flight data recorders, or other debris to piece together the events leading up to the disaster. In these two cases, no such evidence was found. This absence of evidence has led to a range of theories, from the plausible to the fantastical. Some experts have suggested that the planes may have suffered catastrophic structural failures, possibly due to metal fatigue or design flaws in the Avro Tudor IV aircraft. The fact that both planes were part of the same fleet has led some to believe that there could have been a systemic issue with the model that made it prone to failure under certain conditions. However, this theory remains speculative, as no wreckage was ever recovered to confirm or deny it.

Another theory revolves around the idea of navigational errors or fuel mismanagement. Both flights were conducted during a time when navigation relied heavily on radio beacons and manual calculations, and some have suggested that the pilots may have misjudged their positions, leading to fuel exhaustion or disorientation. In the case of the *Star Tiger*, which was flying at a low altitude to avoid headwinds, some have speculated that the aircraft might have encountered unexpected turbulence or downdrafts, causing it to crash into the ocean. However, this does not explain why no wreckage was found, nor does it account for the disappearance of the *Star Ariel*, which was flying at a much higher altitude in perfect weather conditions.

One of the more speculative and popular theories, especially among proponents of the Bermuda Triangle's supernatural reputation, is the idea that both planes fell victim to some unknown force in the Triangle. Over the years, the Bermuda Triangle has been associated with everything from magnetic anomalies to time warps to extraterrestrial activity. Some have suggested that the region contains strong electromagnetic fields that could disrupt navigation instruments or cause sudden mechanical failures. Others have proposed that both planes may have encountered a sudden and unexplained weather phenomenon, such as a "hole in the sky" or a sudden storm that caused them to lose control and crash. These theories, while intriguing, lack scientific evidence and remain firmly in the realm of speculation.

Another theory tied to the Bermuda Triangle's supernatural lore is the possibility of alien abduction. While there is no direct evidence to support this idea, the lack of wreckage or distress signals has led some to suggest that extraterrestrial forces may have been involved in the disappearances. This theory, often dismissed by mainstream scientists and investigators, continues to captivate the public imagination and is frequently featured in documentaries, books, and television shows about the Bermuda Triangle. The idea of alien intervention fits neatly into the broader mythology of the Bermuda Triangle as a place where the normal laws of physics and nature seem to break down.

One of the more grounded theories involves the possibility of sabotage or foul play. Some researchers have speculated that both the *Star Tiger* and *Star Ariel* may have been deliberately brought down by human action, possibly as part of a covert operation or terrorist plot. The post-World War II era was a time of great political tension, and the idea that these planes could have been targeted for sabotage is not entirely out of the realm of possibility. However, there is no concrete evidence to support this theory, and no known groups or individuals ever claimed responsibility for the disappearances. Furthermore, if sabotage had been involved, one might expect some trace of the aircraft to have been found, such as debris or wreckage.

Despite the many theories, the disappearance of the *Star Tiger* and *Star Ariel* remains unsolved to this day. In the years since the incidents, advancements in aviation technology, such as more accurate navigation systems and enhanced search and rescue capabilities, have made similar disappearances far less common. However, the mystery of these two planes continues to haunt those who study the Bermuda Triangle, serving as a reminder of just how little we still understand about this region.

The cases of the *Star Tiger* and *Star Ariel* have left a lasting legacy, not only in aviation history but also in popular culture. These disappearances have been featured in numerous books, documentaries, and television programs about the Bermuda Triangle, often used as prime examples of the region's unexplained phenomena. The lack of any definitive explanation for what happened to these two planes allows them to remain a central part of the Bermuda Triangle's enduring mystery. The loss of the *Star Tiger* and *Star Ariel* continues to fuel speculation, with each new theory adding another layer to the legend of the Bermuda Triangle.

In conclusion, the unsolved case of the *Star Tiger* and *Star Ariel* stands as one of the most compelling mysteries of the Bermuda Triangle. Both planes disappeared under remarkably similar circumstances, leaving no wreckage, no survivors, and no clear explanation for what happened. The disappearances have been the subject of extensive investigation, yet the answers remain elusive. Whether due to navigational errors, mechanical failure, sabotage, or some unknown force within the Bermuda Triangle, the fate of these two planes is likely to remain one of aviation's greatest mysteries for years to come. Their stories contribute to the mythos of the Bermuda Triangle, a place where the boundaries between reality and the unknown blur, captivating our imagination and defying our understanding of the natural world.

Chapter 13: The Science Behind the Mystery

The Bermuda Triangle has fascinated people for decades, and while many attribute its strange occurrences to paranormal forces, aliens, or even mythical cities like Atlantis, there is a significant body of scientific investigation behind the mystery. Researchers have proposed a variety of natural explanations, ranging from environmental factors to human error, for the mysterious disappearances of ships and planes in the area. The Bermuda Triangle, stretching roughly from Miami, Florida, to Bermuda and then to San Juan, Puerto Rico, is one of the most heavily traveled shipping lanes in the world, making it a region where incidents are more likely simply due to the high volume of traffic. Nonetheless, many scientists believe that the strange happenings in the Bermuda Triangle can be attributed to a combination of geographical, oceanic, atmospheric, and human factors.

One of the most prominent scientific explanations for the mystery of the Bermuda Triangle involves the complex geography and environmental conditions of the region. The Triangle lies within an area of the Atlantic Ocean that is affected by strong currents, including the Gulf Stream. The Gulf Stream is a powerful ocean current that flows from the Gulf of Mexico, along the eastern coast of the United States, and across the Atlantic Ocean. The current is known for its speed, which can reach up to 5.6 miles per hour, and its ability to rapidly transport objects or debris from one location to another. This strong current can easily sweep away debris from shipwrecks or plane crashes, making it difficult for search teams to find any remains or wreckage.

In addition to the Gulf Stream, the Bermuda Triangle is also known for its deep underwater trenches. The Puerto Rico Trench, located just outside the Triangle's boundaries, is one of the deepest parts of the Atlantic Ocean, plunging to a depth of nearly 27,500 feet (8,376 meters). This trench, along with other deep underwater features in the region, makes it possible for wreckage from ships or planes to sink quickly and become virtually unrecoverable. Even modern search and rescue operations, equipped with sonar technology and remotely operated vehicles (ROVs), have difficulty exploring such extreme depths. This can explain why many ships and planes that disappear in the Bermuda Triangle are never found, leaving behind no evidence of their fate.

Weather conditions also play a crucial role in the mystery of the Bermuda Triangle. The region is known for its unpredictable and severe weather patterns, which can change rapidly without warning. Sudden storms, powerful winds, and waterspouts are not uncommon in this part of the Atlantic, particularly during hurricane season. Hurricanes are massive tropical storms that form in the Atlantic and can cause immense destruction to ships and planes. In the early days of maritime and aviation history, sailors and pilots lacked the advanced weather forecasting technology we have today, making it more likely that they would encounter unexpected storms or rough seas that could lead to disasters. Even in modern times, with improved weather prediction systems, sudden storms can still catch vessels off guard and cause accidents.

Another atmospheric phenomenon that has been cited as a potential explanation for some of the strange occurrences in the Bermuda Triangle is a concept known as "electronic fog" or St. Elmo's fire. Electronic fog is a meteorological phenomenon where planes or ships are enveloped in a dense, static-charged mist. This fog can interfere with navigational instruments, leading to malfunctions in compasses, radios, and other essential equipment. Some pilots and sailors have reported encountering this fog in the Bermuda Triangle, describing how their instruments suddenly stopped working, making it difficult to navigate or maintain control of their vessels. The cause of electronic fog is not fully understood, but it is believed to be related to the interaction of atmospheric electrical charges with moisture in the air, possibly heightened by the region's frequent thunderstorms. While electronic fog is rare, its potential to disrupt navigation could explain some of the unexplained disappearances in the Bermuda Triangle.

Compass malfunctions are often linked to the Bermuda Triangle, with reports of navigational instruments behaving erratically or pointing in the wrong direction. One theory suggests that the region is home to a magnetic anomaly, where the Earth's magnetic field behaves differently from elsewhere. Compasses typically point toward magnetic north, which differs from true north, but in certain areas, the two align. Historically, sailors have noted that in parts of the Bermuda Triangle, compasses seem to point to true north rather than magnetic north, a phenomenon called "magnetic declination." This could cause navigational errors, leading ships or planes off course. However, modern navigation systems are designed to account for magnetic declination, and it is no longer considered a major risk. Still, compass errors remain part of the Bermuda Triangle lore, and in earlier times, they could have contributed to accidents in the region.

Another scientific theory that has garnered attention involves the possible role of methane hydrate eruptions in the Bermuda Triangle. Methane hydrate is a form of natural gas trapped within the ocean floor. Under certain conditions, large deposits of methane can become destabilized and rapidly release gas bubbles into the water, causing the density of the water to decrease. This phenomenon is sometimes referred to as a "methane blowout." If a ship were to pass through an area where a methane blowout occurred, the reduction in water density could cause the vessel to lose buoyancy and sink suddenly. Similarly, methane gas rising into the atmosphere could affect the engines of low-flying planes, potentially leading to crashes. While methane blowouts are rare, some scientists believe that they could explain certain disappearances within the Bermuda Triangle, especially those involving ships that vanished without sending distress signals.

Another explanation involves oceanic phenomena such as "rogue waves." Rogue waves are unusually large and powerful waves that can appear suddenly in open water, often without warning. These waves are much larger than the surrounding waves and can reach heights of up to 100 feet. Rogue waves are capable of overwhelming even large ships, causing them to capsize or break apart. The Bermuda Triangle's location in the North Atlantic, where powerful storms and ocean currents interact, makes it a region where rogue waves are more likely to occur. In the past, rogue waves were thought to be extremely rare, but recent research has shown that they may be more common than previously believed, particularly in areas with strong oceanic currents like the Bermuda Triangle.

In addition to environmental factors, human error is a significant contributor to accidents in the Bermuda Triangle. Navigational mistakes, miscommunication, and mechanical failures have all played a role in the loss of ships and planes in the region. Many accidents attributed to the Bermuda Triangle have been the result of mundane issues like poor maintenance, insufficient training, or failure to adhere to established safety protocols. In the case of aircraft, for example, inexperienced pilots flying long distances over open water may become disoriented, especially in poor weather conditions. Disorientation, combined with the vastness of the ocean, can lead to deadly consequences if a pilot loses track of their location or altitude.

One of the most famous cases of disorientation in the Bermuda Triangle involves Flight 19, a group of five U.S. Navy torpedo bombers that disappeared during a training exercise in December 1945. The flight, led by an experienced pilot, Lieutenant Charles Taylor, became lost while flying over the Atlantic. Taylor reported that his compass was malfunctioning, and the pilots were unable to determine their position. Despite radio communication with base, the planes eventually ran out of fuel and disappeared. The incident led to a large-scale search and rescue operation, but no trace of the planes or the 14 crew members was ever found. Flight 19's disappearance is often cited as evidence of the Bermuda Triangle's mysterious nature, but many experts believe that the incident was the result of navigational error and pilot disorientation.

Technological advancements have helped reduce the number of accidents in the Bermuda Triangle in recent years. Modern ships and aircraft are equipped with more sophisticated navigation systems, including GPS and satellite communication, which allow for more accurate tracking of their positions. In addition, advances in weather forecasting and monitoring have made it easier to avoid severe storms and other hazardous conditions. These technological improvements have led to a decline in disappearances in the Bermuda Triangle, suggesting that many of the accidents in the region may have been caused by factors that are now better understood and mitigated.

Despite these advancements, the Bermuda Triangle remains a subject of fascination, largely because many of the disappearances remain unsolved. While scientific explanations account for most of the accidents, the lack of concrete evidence in some cases has left room for speculation and alternative theories. For example, some proponents of the paranormal believe that the Bermuda Triangle is home to mysterious energy vortices or gateways to other dimensions. Others suggest that extraterrestrial forces are responsible for the disappearances, possibly abducting ships and planes for unknown purposes. These theories, while not supported by scientific evidence, continue to capture the public's imagination and contribute to the ongoing myth of the Bermuda Triangle.

In conclusion, the science behind the Bermuda Triangle points to a combination of environmental, geographic, and human factors as the primary causes of the accidents and disappearances in the region. Strong ocean currents, deep underwater trenches, sudden storms, rogue waves, and methane hydrate eruptions all contribute to the dangers of the area. Human error, mechanical failure, and navigational issues also play significant roles in many of the incidents. While these scientific explanations account for the majority of accidents, the lack of physical evidence in some cases, combined with the region's reputation for mystery, has allowed more speculative and fantastical theories to persist. The Bermuda Triangle remains an enigmatic part of the world, where science and myth continue to intertwine, and as long as unanswered questions remain, its allure will continue to captivate the imagination of people around the globe.

Chapter 14: The Bermuda Triangle's Underwater Caves

The Bermuda Triangle's underwater caves are one of the most intriguing and lesser-known elements that contribute to the region's enduring mystery. These submerged labyrinths and complex cave systems, hidden deep beneath the ocean's surface, form a significant part of the underwater landscape within the Triangle. These caves are not only remarkable geological formations but are also potentially linked to many of the disappearances and strange occurrences reported in the area. While much of the focus surrounding the Bermuda Triangle is on the disappearance of ships and planes, the underwater geography, including the caves and caverns beneath the sea, plays a key role in shaping the region's mysterious reputation.

The underwater caves in the Bermuda Triangle are primarily located in and around the Bahamas, a region that forms part of the Triangle's western boundary. The Bahamas, famous for their clear blue waters and tropical beauty, are also home to a series of intricate cave systems, some of which extend deep into the ocean. These caves are formed primarily by a process known as karst topography, which occurs when limestone or other soluble rocks are gradually dissolved by water, leaving behind hollow spaces and tunnels. Over thousands of years, this process has created a vast network of underwater caves, sinkholes, and tunnels that stretch beneath the ocean floor.

One of the most famous underwater cave systems in the Bermuda Triangle is the Blue Holes of the Bahamas. These blue holes are large, vertical underwater caves or sinkholes, named for the striking deep blue color they create when viewed from above. The color is the result of the clear water and the extreme depth of the holes, which can reach over 600 feet (182 meters) in some cases. The most well-known of these blue holes is Dean's Blue Hole, located near Long Island in the Bahamas.

It is the second-deepest blue hole in the world, with a depth of 663 feet (202 meters). However, there are many other blue holes scattered throughout the Bahamas, both inland and offshore, each with its own unique characteristics.

The blue holes and underwater caves in the Bermuda Triangle have long been the subject of fascination for divers, scientists, and explorers. These caves are often considered dangerous to explore, not only because of their depth but also due to their complex and often unpredictable structure. Many of these caves have multiple passages and tunnels that twist and turn, creating a maze-like environment that can easily disorient even the most experienced divers. The water in these caves is often crystal clear, but in some cases, it can become murky due to silt or the presence of organic matter, further increasing the risk for divers. The caves can also have strong currents, which can pull divers deeper into the caverns or make it difficult for them to navigate safely.

One of the most intriguing aspects of the Bermuda Triangle's underwater caves is their potential connection to some of the disappearances reported in the region. Some researchers and scientists believe that ships or planes that have vanished in the Bermuda Triangle may have sunk into these deep underwater caverns, making it nearly impossible to locate wreckage or debris. The extreme depth of some of the caves, combined with the powerful ocean currents, could easily pull wreckage into the caves or cause it to be scattered across the ocean floor, making it difficult for search teams to find any trace of the missing vessels. This theory is particularly compelling in cases where no debris or wreckage has ever been found, even after extensive search efforts.

Another possible explanation for the role of underwater caves in the Bermuda Triangle mystery involves methane gas. Some scientists have suggested that the underwater caves and blue holes in the Bahamas could be linked to methane hydrate deposits on the ocean floor. Methane hydrate is a form of natural gas trapped in ice-like structures beneath the sea. When these deposits become destabilized, they can release large amounts of methane gas into the water. This gas could reduce the buoyancy of the water, causing ships to sink rapidly without warning. Additionally, if methane gas were to rise to the surface and into the atmosphere, it could potentially affect the engines of planes flying overhead, leading to crashes. While this theory remains speculative, it provides a possible natural explanation for some of the disappearances in the Bermuda Triangle.

In addition to methane gas, some researchers have explored the possibility that underwater caves in the Bermuda Triangle may be responsible for unusual electromagnetic activity in the region. It is well-documented that the Bermuda Triangle is one of the few places on Earth where compasses sometimes point to true north instead of magnetic north, a phenomenon known as compass variation. While this compass variation is now understood and accounted for by modern navigational systems, in earlier times, it may have led to navigational errors that caused ships and planes to become lost. Some theories suggest that the underwater caves, particularly those containing large amounts of certain minerals or magnetic rocks, could create localized magnetic anomalies that interfere with navigation equipment. These magnetic anomalies could cause compasses to malfunction or planes and ships to become disoriented, leading them off course and into dangerous waters.

The underwater caves of the Bermuda Triangle are also rich in marine life, and this biodiversity has attracted the attention of marine biologists and oceanographers. The caves serve as a habitat for a wide variety of species, including fish, crustaceans, and even some rare or endangered creatures. The unique conditions of these caves, including their depth, lack of sunlight, and varying levels of oxygen, have led to the evolution of species that are specially adapted to survive in these extreme environments. Some of the creatures found in the blue holes and underwater caves are bioluminescent, meaning they produce their own light. This adaptation allows them to navigate the dark cave systems and hunt for prey. The presence of these bioluminescent organisms adds to the eerie, otherworldly atmosphere of the caves, further fueling the mystique of the Bermuda Triangle.

While the scientific study of the Bermuda Triangle's underwater caves has provided valuable insights into the region's geology and biology, it has also raised new questions. Some researchers have proposed that these caves may hold clues to the ancient history of the region, including the possibility that they were once above water during periods of lower sea levels. The Bahamas and the surrounding area were likely part of a larger landmass during the last ice age, when sea levels were much lower than they are today. As the ice melted and sea levels rose, the caves were submerged, creating the underwater labyrinths we see today. This theory suggests that some of the caves may contain fossils, artifacts, or other remnants of ancient civilizations that once inhabited the area. Some proponents of the Atlantis theory, for example, believe that the Bermuda Triangle's underwater caves could hold evidence of a lost civilization that was swallowed by the sea.

Exploration of the Bermuda Triangle's underwater caves has been limited by the challenges of deep-sea diving and the dangers posed by the caves themselves. However, advances in technology, including remotely operated vehicles (ROVs) and underwater drones, have made it possible to explore these caves in greater detail than ever before. ROVs can navigate the narrow passages and tunnels of the caves, capturing video footage and collecting samples without putting human divers at risk. These technological advancements have allowed scientists to map the caves more accurately and study the geology and biology of the region in greater depth. However, the full extent of the underwater cave systems in the Bermuda Triangle remains unknown, and much of the region's underwater landscape has yet to be explored.

In popular culture, the underwater caves of the Bermuda Triangle have often been portrayed as mysterious and dangerous places, filled with hidden dangers and secrets. Some fictional accounts depict the caves as the lair of sea monsters or the entrance to other dimensions. Others suggest that the caves are home to ancient treasure or the remnants of a lost civilization. While these depictions are purely imaginative, they reflect the fascination and intrigue that the Bermuda Triangle and its underwater caves continue to inspire.

In conclusion, the underwater caves of the Bermuda Triangle are a fascinating and complex part of the region's geography. These caves, formed by natural processes over thousands of years, are not only remarkable geological formations but may also hold clues to the many disappearances and strange occurrences that have made the Bermuda Triangle famous. From their role in shaping the ocean currents to their potential connection to methane gas releases and magnetic anomalies, the caves are a critical part of the Bermuda Triangle's mystery. While modern science has provided some answers, much about these underwater labyrinths remains unknown, and as exploration of the region continues, it is possible that the caves will reveal new insights into one of the world's most enduring mysteries.

Chapter 15: The Phantom Lights and Apparitions

The Bermuda Triangle has been the subject of countless strange and unexplained phenomena over the years, and among the most mysterious are reports of phantom lights and ghostly apparitions. These eerie occurrences have been reported by sailors, pilots, and even by entire crews of ships and aircraft, adding another layer of mystique to the legend of the Triangle. While some attribute these sightings to natural phenomena or human error, others believe that they could be evidence of something more paranormal in nature. The stories of phantom lights and apparitions are some of the most compelling in the long history of the Bermuda Triangle, often leaving those who experience them both bewildered and terrified.

One of the most commonly reported phenomena in the Bermuda Triangle involves strange lights that appear in the sky or on the surface of the ocean. These lights are often described as glowing orbs, bright flashes, or streaks of light that move in unnatural ways, sometimes darting across the sky or hovering above the water. In some cases, the lights seem to follow ships or planes for extended periods before suddenly disappearing. Witnesses often report that the lights appear out of nowhere and vanish just as quickly, leaving no trace or explanation for their appearance. These lights have been described in various ways: some as small, flickering lights like candles in the distance, while others as large, pulsating glows that light up the entire horizon.

One famous instance of phantom lights in the Bermuda Triangle occurred in 1973 when Captain Don Henry of the cargo ship *SS Capitana* reported seeing a series of strange lights while sailing through the Triangle. According to Captain Henry, the lights appeared suddenly in the sky, arranged in a triangular formation, and followed the ship for several minutes before disappearing without a trace. The crew of the *SS Capitana* was reportedly shaken by the encounter, and although they attempted to document the lights using onboard instruments, no definitive record of the event was ever captured. This sighting is just one of many similar reports from ships and planes that have passed through the region, each adding to the enigma of the Bermuda Triangle.

Many of the reports of strange lights in the Bermuda Triangle bear a striking resemblance to accounts of Unidentified Flying Objects (UFOs) or extraterrestrial activity. Some people believe that the lights could be evidence of alien encounters, possibly connected to the disappearances of ships and planes in the area. According to this theory, the Bermuda Triangle may serve as a kind of portal or gateway for extraterrestrial visitors, who use the region as a point of entry into Earth's atmosphere. Proponents of this theory point to the recurring descriptions of the lights, which often seem to defy the laws of physics by moving at incredible speeds, making sudden sharp turns, or disappearing in an instant. These characteristics, they argue, suggest that the lights are not natural phenomena but rather advanced technology beyond human understanding.

While the alien theory is popular, scientists and skeptics have proposed more grounded explanations for the strange lights seen in the Bermuda Triangle. One possibility is that the lights are the result of natural atmospheric conditions, such as St. Elmo's fire. St. Elmo's fire is a weather phenomenon in which a visible electrical discharge occurs due to the ionization of air around a ship's mast or an aircraft's wings. This phenomenon can create a glowing effect, often blue or violet, that appears to hover around the edges of objects. St. Elmo's fire has been observed by sailors for centuries and was once considered an omen of bad luck. However, modern science explains it as a natural result of static electricity buildup in certain weather conditions, particularly during thunderstorms or when there is high atmospheric pressure. While St. Elmo's fire could explain some sightings of strange lights, it does not account for all reports, especially those that describe large or fast-moving lights in the sky.

Another potential explanation for the phantom lights is a natural phenomenon known as bioluminescence, which occurs when certain organisms, such as plankton or jellyfish, emit light. In some areas of the ocean, particularly in warmer waters like those of the Bermuda Triangle, bioluminescent organisms are plentiful. When disturbed by ships or waves, these organisms can emit a bright glow that lights up the water around them. This effect can create the appearance of glowing patches on the ocean's surface or even underwater "light shows" that seem to follow ships. While bioluminescence could explain some reports of glowing lights on the ocean, it does not fully account for sightings of lights in the sky or the more complex movements described in many reports.

In addition to strange lights, many people who have passed through the Bermuda Triangle have reported seeing ghostly apparitions or other paranormal entities. These apparitions are often described as shadowy figures, transparent shapes, or even full-bodied spirits that appear on ships or planes without explanation. In some cases, witnesses claim to have seen entire ghost ships, spectral vessels that appear out of the mist before vanishing again. These ghost ships are often described as old-fashioned sailing vessels, seemingly out of place in the modern ocean, and are sometimes seen with no crew on board, drifting silently across the water.

One of the most famous ghost ship stories in the Bermuda Triangle is that of the *Ellen Austin*, a ship that reportedly encountered a mysterious, abandoned vessel while sailing through the region in 1881. According to the story, the crew of the *Ellen Austin* came across the derelict ship, which appeared to be in perfect condition but had no crew on board. The captain of the *Ellen Austin* ordered some of his men to board the ghost ship and sail it alongside their own vessel. However, after a few days, the ghost ship disappeared into the mist, along with the crew members who had been sent to sail it. The ship and the men were never seen again, and the story of the *Ellen Austin* has since become one of the most enduring legends of the Bermuda Triangle.

The apparitions reported in the Bermuda Triangle are not limited to ghost ships. Some sailors and pilots have reported seeing ghostly figures on their own vessels, often appearing in the middle of the night or during times of stress. These apparitions are often described as crew members who vanished or died under mysterious circumstances, returning to haunt the ship or plane. In some cases, the apparitions are said to speak to the living, delivering cryptic messages or warnings before disappearing again. These sightings are often accompanied by a sense of unease or dread, leading some to believe that the Bermuda Triangle is haunted by the spirits of those who have disappeared in the region.

One possible explanation for these ghostly apparitions is the phenomenon of "phantom limb syndrome," which occurs when people experience sensations or even hallucinations related to parts of the body that are no longer there. Similarly, in high-stress situations, the brain can create visual or auditory hallucinations as a coping mechanism. Sailors and pilots who are isolated in the vastness of the ocean or sky for long periods may experience heightened levels of anxiety or exhaustion, which could lead to hallucinations of ghostly figures or strange lights. These hallucinations could be a way for the brain to process fear or confusion, especially in an environment as remote and mysterious as the Bermuda Triangle.

Another potential explanation for ghostly apparitions in the Bermuda Triangle is rooted in the concept of "time slips" or temporal anomalies. According to some paranormal researchers, the Bermuda Triangle may be a location where time itself behaves differently, allowing people to briefly see into the past or the future. This theory suggests that the apparitions seen in the Triangle could be echoes of past events, replaying themselves like a recording. In this view, the ghost ships and figures that appear to sailors and pilots may not be spirits in the traditional sense but rather glimpses of a different time period, visible only because of the unique conditions in the Bermuda Triangle. This theory, while speculative, has gained traction among those who believe that the Triangle is a place where the normal rules of time and space do not apply.

Despite the many theories and explanations, the phantom lights and apparitions of the Bermuda Triangle remain largely unexplained. While natural phenomena like St. Elmo's fire, bioluminescence, and hallucinations could account for some of the sightings, they do not fully explain the scope or variety of experiences reported by those who have encountered strange occurrences in the region. The fact that many of these sightings have been reported by experienced sailors and pilots, who are familiar with the natural conditions of the ocean and the sky, adds to the mystery. These individuals often insist that what they saw was not a natural phenomenon but something far more unusual and inexplicable.

In conclusion, the phantom lights and apparitions of the Bermuda Triangle are among the most eerie and enigmatic aspects of the region's mystery. Whether they are the result of natural phenomena, psychological effects, or something more supernatural, these sightings continue to baffle and intrigue those who experience them. From strange lights that dart across the sky to ghostly figures that appear on ships, these encounters add to the mystique of the Bermuda Triangle and ensure that its legend will continue to capture the imagination of people around the world. As long as these strange occurrences persist, the Bermuda Triangle will remain a place where the line between reality and the unknown is blurred, and where the mysteries of the deep ocean and the skies above continue to inspire awe and fear.

Chapter 16: The Influence of Human Error

The influence of human error plays a significant role in the mysterious incidents and disappearances within the Bermuda Triangle. While many theories about the Bermuda Triangle center around supernatural or unexplained forces such as extraterrestrials, time warps, or paranormal phenomena, a more grounded explanation points to the inevitable impact of human error in both navigation and decision-making. Human error has been responsible for countless accidents throughout history, and when considering the unique and challenging conditions of the Bermuda Triangle—a region known for its unpredictable weather patterns, powerful currents, and vast expanses of open water—mistakes made by sailors, pilots, and navigators can have tragic consequences.

One of the primary factors contributing to human error in the Bermuda Triangle is the sheer difficulty of navigating in this region. The vast expanse of open ocean, with few landmarks or reference points, can make it challenging for even experienced sailors and pilots to stay on course. In the early days of maritime and aviation travel, before the advent of GPS and modern navigation systems, mariners and aviators relied heavily on compasses and other basic tools to determine their position. However, in the Bermuda Triangle, compasses are known to exhibit strange behavior. It is one of the few places on Earth where compasses sometimes point to true north rather than magnetic north, a phenomenon known as compass variation. This anomaly, which occurs due to the Earth's magnetic fields, can cause confusion for those unfamiliar with the region and lead to navigational errors.

Historically, compass malfunction or variation has been linked to several mysterious incidents in the Bermuda Triangle. When compasses deviate from magnetic north, even by a few degrees, it can cause ships and planes to go off course, particularly if the navigator is inexperienced or unaware of the anomaly. In a vast and featureless ocean, a small navigational error can have catastrophic consequences. Without visible landmarks to correct their course, sailors and pilots might continue in the wrong direction for hours or even days, leading them far from their intended path. In some cases, this can result in a vessel becoming hopelessly lost, and in extreme conditions, it could lead to the ship or plane running out of fuel or encountering dangerous weather conditions that it might otherwise have avoided.

In addition to compass variation, the Bermuda Triangle is known for its unpredictable and rapidly changing weather patterns. Sudden storms, waterspouts, and rogue waves are common in the region, particularly during hurricane season. Even in modern times, these weather events can catch experienced sailors and pilots off guard, leading to poor decision-making in moments of crisis. In the early days of ocean exploration and aviation, weather forecasting was far less advanced, and many vessels ventured into the Triangle with little warning of approaching storms. Human error in assessing weather conditions, underestimating the severity of an incoming storm, or failing to take appropriate action can lead to disastrous consequences. In the chaos of a sudden storm, panic can set in, and decisions made under pressure may worsen an already dangerous situation.

Human error is not only confined to navigation or weather assessment but also extends to the operational side of running ships and aircraft. The complex machinery of ships and planes requires constant maintenance and oversight, and even small oversights or misjudgments can lead to mechanical failures. For example, during World War II, the USS *Cyclops*, a Navy cargo ship, disappeared in the Bermuda Triangle with 309 crew members on board. While many theories have been proposed about what happened to the *Cyclops*, ranging from enemy attacks to storms, some researchers believe that human error may have played a role. The ship was heavily loaded with manganese ore, and it is possible that the cargo was improperly distributed, leading to a dangerous imbalance that made the ship more susceptible to capsizing during a storm. Additionally, the ship's engines may have been poorly maintained, which could have contributed to a mechanical failure at a critical moment.

Similarly, the SS *Marine Sulphur Queen*, an American tanker that disappeared in the Bermuda Triangle in 1963, was carrying molten sulfur, a highly volatile substance. Investigations into the ship's disappearance revealed that it had been poorly maintained and may have been structurally unsound. Leaks in the tanks carrying the molten sulfur could have caused an explosion or fire on board, contributing to the ship's demise. In both cases, human error—whether in the loading of cargo, maintenance of the vessel, or failure to address known risks—likely played a critical role in the disappearance of these ships. These incidents highlight the dangers of human oversight in ensuring that vessels are seaworthy and capable of safely navigating the challenging conditions of the Bermuda Triangle.

Aviation accidents in the Bermuda Triangle also often involve human error, particularly in terms of miscommunication, misjudgment, or disorientation. One of the most famous examples is the disappearance of Flight 19, a squadron of five U.S. Navy torpedo bombers that vanished during a training mission in December 1945. The flight was led by Lieutenant Charles Taylor, an experienced pilot who became disoriented after his compass malfunctioned. Despite radio contact with ground control, Taylor was unable to determine the squadron's position and made several critical errors in judgment that led the planes farther out to sea. Eventually, the squadron ran out of fuel and likely crashed into the ocean, though the wreckage was never found. Human error, both in terms of navigational mistakes and decision-making under stress, played a key role in the loss of Flight 19.

Disorientation, often referred to as spatial disorientation, is a common problem for pilots, particularly when flying over featureless expanses of water or in poor visibility conditions. The Bermuda Triangle, with its vast stretches of open ocean, can create the perfect environment for this type of confusion. Without clear visual references such as the horizon or landmarks, a pilot can easily lose track of their altitude, speed, or direction, especially if their instruments are malfunctioning or they are inexperienced. This can lead to poor decision-making, such as flying in the wrong direction or at an unsafe altitude, increasing the risk of a crash. Spatial disorientation has been cited as a contributing factor in several disappearances within the Bermuda Triangle, and in some cases, the pilot's disorientation may have been compounded by fatigue, stress, or lack of training.

In the age of modern technology, human error still plays a significant role in accidents and incidents in the Bermuda Triangle. While GPS and advanced navigation systems have reduced the likelihood of getting lost, they are not foolproof, and human operators must still interpret and act on the information provided by these systems. Mistakes in interpreting radar data, miscalculating fuel levels, or failing to follow proper protocols can still lead to accidents. In some cases, overreliance on technology can create a false sense of security, leading pilots or captains to make risky decisions that they might not have made if they were more cautious or aware of their surroundings. This reliance on technology can also result in complacency, where basic navigational skills or safety procedures are neglected.

One of the major contributors to human error is the psychological impact of stress and fatigue on decision-making. The open ocean is a stressful environment, particularly when conditions become challenging or dangerous. Sailors and pilots who spend long hours at sea or in the air are subject to physical and mental fatigue, which can impair their ability to think clearly and make sound decisions. Fatigue can lead to mistakes in judgment, slower reaction times, and difficulty in processing complex information. In moments of crisis, such as during a sudden storm or mechanical failure, fatigue can exacerbate the situation, leading to panic and poor decision-making. In the Bermuda Triangle, where conditions can change rapidly, the ability to remain calm and make rational decisions is critical to survival. However, human error is often magnified by the stress of the moment, leading to disastrous consequences.

Another important aspect of human error in the Bermuda Triangle involves miscommunication or breakdowns in communication between crew members, or between the vessel and those on shore. In some cases, accidents and disappearances could have been avoided if better communication had been maintained. For example, during the disappearance of Flight 19, radio communication between the pilots and ground control became increasingly fragmented as the situation worsened. Misunderstandings about their position and the course they should take contributed to their disorientation. Similarly, ships that encounter mechanical problems or dangerous weather conditions in the Bermuda Triangle may fail to send distress signals in time, either due to equipment failure or human error. In some cases, crews may hesitate to issue a distress call, believing they can resolve the situation on their own, only to realize too late that they need assistance.

Human error is also evident in the planning and execution of voyages through the Bermuda Triangle. In some cases, ships or planes may enter the region without sufficient preparation, such as inadequate fuel reserves, poor weather planning, or lack of proper safety equipment. Overconfidence or disregard for potential dangers can lead to risky decisions, such as attempting to sail through a storm or flying at an unsafe altitude. In other cases, human error may involve misjudging the capabilities of the vessel or aircraft, overloading it with cargo, or failing to conduct proper maintenance checks before departure. These oversights can compound the risks of navigating the Bermuda Triangle and increase the likelihood of an accident or disappearance.

In conclusion, while many theories have been proposed to explain the mystery of the Bermuda Triangle, the influence of human error is one of the most plausible and significant factors. Navigational mistakes, poor decision-making, mechanical failures, and miscommunication all contribute to the accidents and disappearances in the region. The challenging and often unpredictable conditions of the Bermuda Triangle, combined with the psychological and physical demands placed on sailors and pilots, make human error an unavoidable part of the equation. While modern technology has reduced some of the risks associated with navigating the Bermuda Triangle, human error remains a critical factor in understanding the region's enduring mystery. As long as people continue to travel through the Bermuda Triangle, the potential for human error will remain, ensuring that this enigmatic area will continue to be a source of fascination and speculation for years to come.

Chapter 17: The Impact of the Gulf Stream

The Gulf Stream, one of the most powerful and well-known ocean currents in the world, plays a significant role in shaping both the weather and the oceanic conditions in the Bermuda Triangle. This warm Atlantic Ocean current, which flows from the Gulf of Mexico along the eastern coast of the United States before veering out across the Atlantic toward Europe, has long fascinated scientists and mariners alike. Its tremendous speed and strength make it a force of nature that has a profound impact on everything from local weather patterns to global climate, and its influence within the Bermuda Triangle is often seen as one of the primary factors contributing to the region's reputation for mysterious disappearances.

One of the key characteristics of the Gulf Stream is its ability to move water at a tremendous rate. The current can travel at speeds of up to 5.6 miles per hour, which is much faster than most other ocean currents. For sailors and ships navigating through the Bermuda Triangle, this means that even slight miscalculations in navigation can lead to significant changes in position. A ship or plane that drifts into the Gulf Stream can be carried miles off course in a short period, sometimes without the crew even realizing it. In a vast, featureless expanse of ocean, such displacements can lead to confusion, disorientation, and eventually disaster. It's easy to see how the Gulf Stream, with its relentless push, could have contributed to many of the lost vessels and aircraft that have disappeared in the Bermuda Triangle over the centuries.

For example, if a ship is damaged or experiences engine failure while caught in the Gulf Stream, it can quickly be swept far from its last known position, making it difficult for rescue teams to locate it. Even in modern times, search and rescue operations in the Bermuda

Triangle are hampered by the strong current, which can scatter debris over a wide area and push lifeboats or wreckage miles away from the actual site of the accident. This powerful current adds another layer of difficulty to an already challenging environment, where the vastness of the open ocean makes locating lost vessels akin to finding a needle in a haystack. The Gulf Stream, in this way, plays an indirect but vital role in many of the unsolved mysteries of the Bermuda Triangle.

The Gulf Stream's impact on weather patterns in the Bermuda Triangle is another critical factor to consider. Warm water from the Gulf Stream evaporates quickly, feeding moisture into the atmosphere and contributing to the formation of powerful storms. In fact, the warm waters of the Gulf Stream are one of the primary factors responsible for the development and intensification of hurricanes in the Atlantic. These storms, which frequently form in the tropical regions near the Bermuda Triangle, can grow in intensity as they pass over the warm waters of the Gulf Stream, turning from small tropical depressions into full-fledged hurricanes in a matter of hours. Ships and planes caught in these rapidly intensifying storms may have little time to react, especially if the storm forms suddenly and grows stronger faster than expected.

The Bermuda Triangle has long been associated with reports of sudden, violent storms that appear without warning. Many of these storms are likely fueled by the warm waters of the Gulf Stream, which can create localized weather conditions that are both unpredictable and dangerous. Pilots and sailors passing through the region have reported encountering clear skies one minute, only to be engulfed by a powerful storm the next. The Gulf Stream, with its constant supply of warm, moisture-laden air, can make these sudden shifts in weather more likely, contributing to the area's reputation for unpredictable and treacherous conditions. Ships and planes caught in such storms may experience mechanical failures, loss of communication, or disorientation, leading to accidents and disappearances.

The Gulf Stream also creates unique and challenging sea conditions that can be hazardous for vessels navigating through the Bermuda Triangle. The current interacts with other oceanic features, such as the continental shelf, underwater ridges, and deep-sea trenches, creating areas of turbulence, strong eddies, and sudden changes in sea level. Ships passing through these regions may encounter rough seas, with waves reaching significant heights in a short period. In extreme cases, rogue waves—massive, unexpected waves that appear seemingly out of nowhere—can form in areas where the Gulf Stream interacts with other currents or underwater features. These rogue waves have been known to capsize even large ships, and they are one of the many natural hazards that sailors face when navigating the waters of the Bermuda Triangle.

In addition to rogue waves, the Gulf Stream can create dangerous conditions for small boats and pleasure craft that venture into the Bermuda Triangle. The strong current can make it difficult for smaller vessels to maintain their course, especially if they are underpowered or not designed to handle rough seas. Many of the disappearances in the Bermuda Triangle involve small boats that may have been overwhelmed by the fast-moving current or rough conditions created by the interaction of the Gulf Stream with other oceanic forces. Inexperienced sailors, in particular, may find themselves unprepared for the challenges posed by the Gulf Stream, leading to accidents or even the total loss of their vessels.

Another important aspect of the Gulf Stream's influence in the Bermuda Triangle is its ability to affect the water temperature in the region. The warm waters of the Gulf Stream create a sharp contrast with the cooler waters that surround it, particularly as it moves further north along the eastern coast of the United States. This temperature difference can create areas of instability in the atmosphere, leading to the formation of sudden squalls, thunderstorms, or even waterspouts—tornadoes that form over the ocean. These localized weather phenomena can be extremely dangerous for ships and planes passing through the Bermuda Triangle, as they often occur without much warning and can cause significant damage. Waterspouts, in particular, have been reported by sailors and pilots in the region and are known to have enough power to capsize small boats or disrupt the flight paths of aircraft.

The Gulf Stream also plays a crucial role in shaping the ecology of the Bermuda Triangle. The warm waters of the current support a rich and diverse marine ecosystem, attracting a variety of sea life, including fish, dolphins, whales, and sea turtles. This abundance of marine life has made the Bermuda Triangle a popular destination for fishing and recreational boating, as well as scientific research. However, the presence of large marine animals can also pose a hazard to ships and planes passing through the area. Collisions with whales or other large sea creatures have been known to cause damage to vessels, particularly in the days before modern sonar and navigation systems were available. While such collisions are rare, they are another factor that sailors must consider when navigating the Gulf Stream and the waters of the Bermuda Triangle.

The Gulf Stream's fast-moving waters can also complicate rescue operations in the event of a disaster. When a ship or plane goes down in the Bermuda Triangle, the Gulf Stream can quickly carry wreckage, debris, and survivors far from the site of the accident. This makes it difficult for search and rescue teams to locate the wreckage or recover bodies, contributing to the mystery surrounding many of the disappearances in the region. In some cases, the strong current may carry debris hundreds of miles from the original site, making it almost impossible to determine what happened. The Gulf Stream's ability to disperse debris over a wide area is one of the reasons why many ships and planes that have disappeared in the Bermuda Triangle have never been found.

For those who study the ocean and its currents, the Gulf Stream represents a fascinating and complex system that has a profound impact on the environment of the Bermuda Triangle. While its role in the mysterious disappearances of ships and planes may be more subtle than the dramatic theories involving extraterrestrials or paranormal forces, the influence of the Gulf Stream is undeniable. Its powerful currents, its ability to shape weather patterns, and its effect on navigation all contribute to the challenges of safely traversing the Bermuda Triangle. For centuries, sailors and explorers have respected the power of the Gulf Stream, knowing that while it can speed their journey along the coast, it can also sweep them far off course or into dangerous waters if they are not careful.

In addition to its influence on the local environment, the Gulf Stream is a key player in the global climate system. By transporting warm water from the tropics to higher latitudes, the Gulf Stream helps to regulate the climate of the North Atlantic and Western Europe. This process, known as thermohaline circulation, is critical to maintaining the balance of heat in the Earth's oceans and atmosphere. Without the Gulf Stream, the climate of Europe would be much colder, and the weather patterns of the entire Atlantic basin would be dramatically different. This global significance of the Gulf Stream adds another layer of complexity to the role it plays in the Bermuda Triangle, as the current is not just a local phenomenon but part of a much larger system that affects weather and climate on a planetary scale.

Despite the many dangers associated with the Gulf Stream, it is also a vital resource for maritime trade and travel. Ships that catch the current can significantly reduce their travel time, as the fast-moving waters carry them swiftly along the coast and across the Atlantic. This has been true for centuries, dating back to the days of early explorers who relied on the Gulf Stream to speed their journeys from the Americas to Europe. Even today, modern shipping routes take advantage of the Gulf Stream to reduce fuel consumption and travel time, making it an essential part of the global shipping industry. However, sailors must remain vigilant, as the same current that speeds their journey can also sweep them off course or into dangerous waters if they are not careful.

In conclusion, the Gulf Stream is a powerful and complex force that plays a significant role in the environment of the Bermuda Triangle. Its fast-moving currents, ability to influence weather patterns, and impact on navigation all contribute to the challenges of safely traveling through the region. While the Gulf Stream is not solely responsible for the mysterious disappearances of ships and planes in the Bermuda Triangle, it is undoubtedly a key factor that must be considered. The current's influence on the ocean, the atmosphere, and the creatures that inhabit the region make it a critical part of the Bermuda Triangle's unique and enigmatic environment. As long as people continue to sail and fly through these waters, the Gulf Stream will remain a powerful force to be reckoned with, both as a potential hazard and as a vital resource for those who know how to navigate its challenges.

Chapter 18: The Survival Stories from the Bermuda Triangle

The Bermuda Triangle is known for its strange and mysterious disappearances, but there have also been accounts of incredible survival stories from people who lived to tell the tale. These survival stories offer a glimpse into the sometimes terrifying, yet extraordinary, experiences of those who managed to escape the clutches of the so-called "Devil's Triangle." These narratives help balance the darker myths surrounding the region, showing that not everyone who ventures into this dangerous part of the Atlantic Ocean disappears forever. In fact, some of the most thrilling accounts come from survivors who faced everything from mechanical malfunctions to mysterious weather phenomena but still managed to make it out alive, often with tales of the unexplained.

One of the most famous survival stories from the Bermuda Triangle is that of Bruce Gernon, a pilot who flew his Beechcraft Bonanza through the area in December 1970. Gernon was on a routine flight from Andros Island in the Bahamas to Palm Beach, Florida, a trip that he had made many times before without incident. But on this particular flight, Gernon encountered something so strange that it has puzzled him and others for decades. As Gernon approached the Bermuda Triangle, he saw what he described as a strange cloud formation ahead. This was no ordinary cloud; it was shaped like a tunnel, and he had no choice but to fly through it. As Gernon entered the tunnel-like cloud, the aircraft's instruments began malfunctioning, and he felt a strange sense of weightlessness. The walls of the tunnel seemed to close in on him, and electric-like flashes appeared around the aircraft.

For several minutes, Gernon and his passengers were engulfed in this bizarre, swirling cloud. Then, suddenly, they were out of it and back in clear skies. But when Gernon looked at his instruments, he realized something even stranger had happened. Although the flight from Andros Island to Palm Beach typically took 75 minutes, they had made the journey in just 47 minutes—a feat that should have been impossible. It was as if they had traveled through time or space in some inexplicable way. Gernon later dubbed this experience "electronic fog," a mysterious phenomenon that has been linked to other Bermuda Triangle incidents. His story remains one of the most well-known survival accounts connected to the Bermuda Triangle, fueling theories about time warps, vortexes, and distortions in space-time within the region.

Another remarkable survival story comes from the crew of the U.S. Navy ship USS Fogg during World War II. In 1944, the USS Fogg was operating in the North Atlantic near the Bermuda Triangle when it was hit by a German U-boat torpedo. The ship was severely damaged, and a portion of it sank into the sea. Despite the chaos, the surviving crew members were able to keep the ship afloat long enough for rescue teams to arrive. However, what makes this story particularly interesting is what some crew members reported seeing during their ordeal. Several sailors claimed to have witnessed strange lights in the sky, which they could not identify. These lights were not consistent with aircraft or any known technology of the time. The men who survived this harrowing experience were left with unanswered questions about what they had seen, and their accounts added another layer of mystery to the Bermuda Triangle's already strange reputation.

In another extraordinary case, British businessman and pilot Captain Don Henry found himself face-to-face with the dangers of the Bermuda Triangle in 1975. Henry was flying his twin-engine Cessna 402 from Fort Lauderdale to the Bahamas when he encountered sudden engine trouble. The aircraft's engines sputtered and began losing power, forcing Henry to make an emergency landing in the ocean. As his plane hit the water, Henry and his passenger had to quickly exit the aircraft and deploy a life raft. Stranded in the middle of the ocean, surrounded by nothing but endless water, Henry and his passenger were at the mercy of the elements. To make matters worse, a storm was approaching, and the waves grew increasingly violent.

The two men drifted for hours, battling exhaustion, dehydration, and fear as they waited for rescue. Miraculously, after several grueling hours adrift, they were spotted by a passing freighter, which plucked them from the water and brought them to safety. Henry's story of survival in the Bermuda Triangle is a testament to the dangers that the region poses, but also to the resilience of those who manage to survive its perils. His experience added to the growing body of evidence that something about the Bermuda Triangle's waters is unpredictable and dangerous, whether due to natural or mysterious causes.

Another compelling survival story comes from the crew of the American schooner *Patricia* in 1881. The schooner was on a voyage through the Bermuda Triangle when it encountered an unexpected and violent storm. The storm appeared almost out of nowhere, with no prior warning signs. It was so powerful that the schooner's sails were shredded, and the crew struggled to keep the vessel from capsizing. For days, they fought the relentless waves, barely managing to keep the schooner afloat. The crew members were terrified, certain that they would be the next victims of the Bermuda Triangle's infamous reputation.

What made the situation even more frightening were the strange phenomena they reported during the storm. Several crew members claimed to have seen ghostly apparitions in the distance—what they described as "phantom ships" on the horizon. Others reported hearing strange, disembodied voices carried on the wind. Despite the eerie experiences, the crew of the *Patricia* managed to survive the storm and eventually make it to port. Their story was reported in several newspapers of the time, and the mysterious sightings they experienced have since been linked to the legends and lore surrounding the Bermuda Triangle.

Yet another survivor, Joshua Slocum, the first person to sail solo around the world, had his own mysterious experience while sailing through the Bermuda Triangle. Slocum was an experienced sailor who had successfully navigated the globe, yet even he encountered strange phenomena while passing through the Triangle in the early 1900s. Slocum's account is less dramatic in terms of danger but no less mysterious. While sailing in calm waters, he reported being visited by a strange and unexplainable presence onboard his ship. Slocum described feeling as though someone or something was watching him and even claimed that his boat's navigation seemed to be influenced by an invisible force. Though he made it through the Bermuda Triangle unharmed, Slocum's experience has been cited as one of the eerie encounters that add to the Triangle's enigmatic nature.

A more recent case of survival from the Bermuda Triangle occurred in 1991 when professional diver and treasure hunter John Baldwin went missing while exploring a shipwreck in the area. Baldwin had been diving on the wreck of a sunken ship just off the coast of Bermuda when he vanished without a trace. His diving team conducted an exhaustive search, but after several days, hope began to fade. Then, incredibly, after 48 hours, Baldwin was found alive, drifting in the open ocean. When questioned about his disappearance, Baldwin had no clear memory of what had happened. He remembered starting the dive but had no recollection of how he ended up separated from his team and adrift in the middle of the sea. His survival was hailed as a miracle, but it also deepened the mystery of the Bermuda Triangle, as Baldwin's story hinted at the possibility of sudden disorientation or otherworldly forces at play.

The survival stories from the Bermuda Triangle serve as a counterbalance to the tragic tales of disappearance. While many ships and planes have vanished without a trace, these survivors offer hope and a reminder that not all encounters with the Triangle end in tragedy. Some have lived to tell their extraordinary stories, which often include encounters with bizarre weather phenomena, unexplainable malfunctions, and strange, inexplicable occurrences. These accounts only deepen the mystery surrounding the region, as they suggest that while danger may lurk in the waters of the Bermuda Triangle, it is not entirely inescapable.

Many of these survival stories also underscore the role of luck and sheer willpower. Pilots like Bruce Gernon and sailors like Don Henry may have encountered forces they couldn't fully explain, but they also demonstrated incredible calm and resourcefulness in the face of danger. Whether it was through careful navigation, quick thinking, or simply being in the right place at the right time for a rescue, these survivors managed to escape the Bermuda Triangle's grip, leaving behind tantalizing questions about what, exactly, they encountered.

The survival stories also fuel speculation about the nature of the Bermuda Triangle itself. Some argue that these stories provide evidence of natural explanations, such as sudden storms, powerful ocean currents, or magnetic anomalies that can lead to confusion and disorientation. Others believe that the unexplained elements of these stories—such as strange lights, ghostly apparitions, or time distortions—suggest something more mysterious at work, perhaps even paranormal or extraterrestrial forces. Whatever the explanation, these survival stories continue to captivate the public's imagination, offering glimpses into a place where the boundaries of reality and mystery blur.

In conclusion, the survival stories from the Bermuda Triangle are as fascinating and complex as the disappearances that have made the region infamous. They provide valuable insights into the dangers that sailors and pilots face when navigating these treacherous waters, while also raising questions about the unexplained phenomena that seem to occur within its boundaries. Whether driven by luck, skill, or perhaps something beyond human understanding, the people who have survived the Bermuda Triangle's dangers have left behind stories that add to the enigma of this mysterious part of the world.

Chapter 19: The Government Investigations

Government investigations into the Bermuda Triangle have been a key aspect in attempting to uncover the truth behind the mysterious disappearances and strange occurrences reported in the region. Over the years, various governmental agencies, both in the United States and other countries, have looked into the phenomena associated with the Bermuda Triangle, trying to determine whether the dangers posed by this area of the Atlantic Ocean are natural or something more mysterious. These investigations often stem from public pressure, especially after high-profile disappearances of aircraft and ships, such as the USS *Cyclops*, Flight 19, and others. Despite these efforts, the findings from official inquiries have often been inconclusive, leaving the Bermuda Triangle enigma unsolved but offering a more grounded perspective on what might be happening within the Triangle.

The Bermuda Triangle covers a large area of the western Atlantic, bounded roughly by Miami, Bermuda, and Puerto Rico. Its history of strange disappearances dates back centuries, and as more incidents piled up, the U.S. government eventually stepped in to study the problem. One of the earliest and most significant investigations came from the U.S. Navy and Coast Guard. Following the disappearance of Flight 19 in 1945, which involved five U.S. Navy torpedo bombers vanishing during a routine training mission, both branches of the military launched an extensive search-and-rescue operation. This was one of the largest searches of its kind, involving hundreds of ships and aircraft, but it turned up nothing—no wreckage, no survivors, not even a clue as to what happened. This baffling event spurred further inquiries, as the public and military officials alike were desperate for answers.

Flight 19's disappearance prompted the Navy to look more closely at whether there was anything unusual about the area within the Bermuda Triangle. The Navy's official stance has been that there is no extraordinary mystery behind the disappearances, attributing them to navigational errors, human mistakes, and bad weather. In the case of Flight 19, for example, the lead pilot was believed to have been disoriented, possibly due to poor visibility and faulty compass readings. Official records suggested that the aircraft likely ran out of fuel and crashed into the ocean. However, the lack of debris or bodies fueled conspiracy theories, and this case remains one of the most frequently cited in Bermuda Triangle lore. Despite the Navy's official position, public fascination with the Bermuda Triangle persisted, and many people continued to believe that something beyond human understanding was at play.

The U.S. Coast Guard has also been deeply involved in investigating incidents within the Bermuda Triangle. Over the years, the Coast Guard has responded to numerous distress calls from ships and planes in the area, often launching search-and-rescue missions under dire conditions. Their official reports, however, have consistently downplayed any notion of paranormal or extraterrestrial activity. Like the Navy, the Coast Guard attributes most incidents to environmental factors, such as severe weather, rapidly changing ocean currents, and mechanical failure. The Gulf Stream, a powerful and fast-moving ocean current, runs through the Bermuda Triangle and has been cited by both the Coast Guard and Navy as a likely contributor to many of the disappearances. The Gulf Stream can carry debris and wreckage far from its original location, making it incredibly difficult for search teams to locate missing vessels or aircraft. Additionally, the weather in this region can be unpredictable, with violent storms forming quickly, often without warning. Such natural hazards, in the eyes of government officials, provide a sufficient explanation for many of the disappearances.

In the 1970s, further investigations were launched in response to the growing media attention around the Bermuda Triangle. In 1975, the U.S. Navy produced a detailed study on the disappearances, aiming to dispel the myths surrounding the Triangle. The report reviewed over 100 disappearances attributed to the Bermuda Triangle and concluded that there was nothing unusual about the rate of incidents in the area. According to the Navy, the number of missing ships and planes in the Bermuda Triangle was no higher than in any other heavily trafficked area of the world. This finding suggested that the so-called "mystery" of the Bermuda Triangle was more a product of sensationalism than reality. While this report offered a logical explanation, it did little to quell public curiosity or belief in supernatural causes.

The National Transportation Safety Board (NTSB) has also played a role in investigating certain Bermuda Triangle incidents, especially those involving commercial aircraft. In the case of the SS *Marine Sulphur Queen*, a tanker that disappeared in 1963 with 39 crew members onboard, the NTSB conducted a thorough investigation. The ship, which was carrying a cargo of molten sulfur, vanished without a trace after sending its last radio communication near the Bermuda Triangle. Despite an extensive search operation, no wreckage was ever found. The NTSB's investigation concluded that structural issues with the vessel, combined with bad weather, were the most likely cause of the disaster. The tanker was known to have had multiple safety violations, and it was speculated that these weaknesses made the ship vulnerable to sinking during a storm. However, as with many other cases in the Bermuda Triangle, the lack of definitive evidence left room for speculation and conspiracy theories.

In the late 1990s, the National Oceanic and Atmospheric Administration (NOAA) conducted its own analysis of the Bermuda Triangle. NOAA is responsible for monitoring oceanic and atmospheric conditions, and their experts weighed in on the environmental factors that could contribute to the incidents.

According to NOAA, the Bermuda Triangle is located in an area prone to hurricanes, tropical storms, and waterspouts—an unusual meteorological phenomenon where a tornado-like vortex forms over water. These extreme weather events can pose serious threats to ships and aircraft. NOAA also emphasized the role of rogue waves, which are massive, sudden swells of water that can reach heights of 100 feet or more. These waves have the power to capsize ships and disable aircraft, making them a potential explanation for some of the disappearances.

NOAA's findings echoed those of the Navy and Coast Guard, dismissing the need for supernatural explanations. Instead, they pointed to natural phenomena like methane hydrate eruptions on the ocean floor, which could theoretically cause ships to sink rapidly without a trace. Methane hydrates are pockets of gas trapped beneath the ocean floor, and when they erupt, they can reduce the water's density, causing ships to lose buoyancy and sink almost instantly. Although there is no definitive proof that this has happened within the Bermuda Triangle, it remains a plausible theory that the government has considered.

Beyond the United States, other governments have also taken an interest in the Bermuda Triangle, particularly those with territories or shipping routes within its boundaries. The British government, for example, launched an inquiry following the mysterious disappearance of two British South American Airways planes—Star Tiger and Star Ariel—in 1948 and 1949, respectively. Both planes vanished while flying over the Bermuda Triangle, and extensive search efforts turned up no wreckage. The British investigation, much like the U.S. inquiries, concluded that the disappearances were likely due to a combination of navigational errors and bad weather, though the mystery was never fully solved.

While these government investigations have largely debunked the idea of the Bermuda Triangle as a supernatural or extraterrestrial hotspot, they have not fully eliminated the region's mystique. Many people remain convinced that something unusual is happening within the Triangle, whether it be a magnetic anomaly, a time warp, or alien intervention. These theories have been fueled by the fact that in many cases, no wreckage or bodies have been found, even after exhaustive searches. The lack of tangible evidence, combined with strange occurrences like compasses malfunctioning and reports of unusual lights in the sky, has kept the Bermuda Triangle firmly entrenched in the realm of mystery and speculation.

One of the key limitations of these government investigations is that they often focus on individual cases rather than the broader phenomenon. Each incident is typically investigated in isolation, which means that any potential patterns or connections between disappearances might be overlooked. Additionally, the focus of government inquiries is usually on finding logical, natural explanations—such as human error or weather conditions—which can sometimes leave more mysterious elements of the cases unexamined. For example, in the case of Flight 19, the focus was primarily on pilot error, but the reports of malfunctioning instruments and strange radio transmissions were not given the same level of scrutiny.

Some have criticized the government for not doing more to investigate the broader phenomenon of the Bermuda Triangle. Conspiracy theorists, in particular, have suggested that the government may be covering up what is truly happening in the region. They point to the fact that many government reports are heavily redacted or classified, which they believe indicates that the authorities know more than they are letting on. While there is no concrete evidence to support these claims, the secrecy surrounding certain investigations has only fueled suspicion.

In conclusion, government investigations into the Bermuda Triangle have provided valuable insights into many of the incidents associated with the region. However, these inquiries have largely downplayed the more mysterious aspects of the Triangle, focusing instead on logical explanations like human error, mechanical failure, and extreme weather conditions. While these explanations may account for many of the disappearances, they do not fully satisfy the public's curiosity or desire for answers. The Bermuda Triangle remains an enduring mystery, in part because official investigations have not been able to provide conclusive explanations for every incident. As long as there are unanswered questions, the legend of the Bermuda Triangle will continue to captivate and intrigue, even in the face of government efforts to demystify it.

Chapter 20: The Truth Behind the Supernatural Claims

The Bermuda Triangle has long been associated with supernatural claims, fueled by reports of mysterious disappearances, strange phenomena, and unexplained events that have captured the public's imagination for decades. The area, which stretches across the western part of the North Atlantic Ocean between Miami, Bermuda, and Puerto Rico, has become a symbol of fear, intrigue, and wonder. As countless planes, ships, and even submarines have disappeared under bizarre and unexplained circumstances, people have often turned to supernatural explanations to make sense of these occurrences. These claims include everything from alien abductions and time warps to ghost ships and underwater civilizations. While these stories have often been dismissed by scientists and skeptics, the supernatural theories surrounding the Bermuda Triangle have become an inseparable part of its legend, continuing to raise questions about whether there could be truth behind these otherworldly ideas.

One of the most enduring supernatural claims associated with the Bermuda Triangle is the theory of alien abductions. Proponents of this theory suggest that extraterrestrial beings are responsible for the disappearances of ships and planes within the Triangle. This idea gained traction in the mid-20th century, particularly after the disappearance of Flight 19, a group of five U.S. Navy bombers that vanished during a training mission in 1945. Despite extensive search efforts, neither the planes nor the crew were ever found, leading some to believe that they had been taken by aliens. Those who support this theory point to strange radio transmissions recorded before the planes disappeared, in which one of the pilots reportedly said, "We are entering white water, nothing seems right. We don't know where we are, the water is green, no white." This cryptic message, combined with the fact that no wreckage was ever recovered, fueled speculation that the planes had been abducted by extraterrestrial forces.

Alien abduction theorists also cite other instances of strange sightings and experiences within the Bermuda Triangle as evidence of extraterrestrial activity. There have been numerous reports of unidentified flying objects (UFOs) seen hovering over the Triangle, as well as claims of strange lights in the sky or objects moving at incredible speeds. Some believe that these UFOs are conducting surveillance of Earth or are using the Bermuda Triangle as a portal for interdimensional travel. While there is no concrete evidence to support the alien abduction theory, it remains one of the most popular supernatural explanations for the Bermuda Triangle's mysteries. The idea of alien intervention taps into humanity's fascination with the unknown and the possibility of life beyond Earth, making it a compelling narrative for those seeking answers to the Bermuda Triangle's enigma.

Another common supernatural theory tied to the Bermuda Triangle is the idea of time warps or dimensional shifts. According to this theory, the Bermuda Triangle is a location where the fabric of time and space is unstable, allowing for the possibility of time travel or movement between parallel dimensions. This concept is often linked to reports of compasses spinning out of control or aircraft and ships vanishing without a trace, as if they had been transported to another time or place. One of the most famous proponents of this theory is pilot Bruce Gernon, who claimed to have experienced a "time tunnel" while flying through the Bermuda Triangle in 1970. Gernon reported that he encountered a strange, tunnel-shaped cloud that seemed to pull his plane into it. As he flew through the cloud, the aircraft's instruments malfunctioned, and he experienced a sensation of weightlessness. When Gernon emerged from the tunnel, he discovered that he had traveled 100 miles in just a few minutes, far faster than should have been possible. He believed that he had passed through a time warp, which had somehow allowed him to cover the distance in an impossibly short time.

The time warp theory is often associated with the idea of "electronic fog," a mysterious phenomenon where planes and ships encounter a thick, fog-like substance that causes navigational equipment to malfunction. Those who support the time warp theory suggest that this fog is a sign of a rift in the space-time continuum, which may be responsible for the disappearances in the Bermuda Triangle. While this idea may sound like science fiction, it has gained traction among some researchers and theorists who believe that the Bermuda Triangle may be a unique area where the laws of physics behave differently. However, mainstream scientists have been skeptical of these claims, pointing out that there is no empirical evidence to support the existence of time warps or dimensional shifts.

Another supernatural claim often linked to the Bermuda Triangle is the theory of an underwater city or civilization, most notably Atlantis. The legend of Atlantis, an advanced civilization that supposedly sank beneath the ocean thousands of years ago, has been a part of human mythology since ancient times. Some believe that the Bermuda Triangle is the location of the lost city of Atlantis and that its powerful, unknown technology may be responsible for the strange occurrences in the area. This theory suggests that the Atlanteans possessed advanced technology, such as energy crystals or anti-gravity devices, that could be affecting modern-day ships and planes passing over the region. Some versions of this theory propose that the remains of Atlantis lie deep beneath the ocean floor and that these ancient technologies are still active, creating the mysterious disappearances and electromagnetic anomalies associated with the Bermuda Triangle.

While the Atlantis theory has been widely dismissed by historians and archaeologists, it remains a popular idea in the realm of paranormal research. There have been claims of sonar images revealing unusual structures on the ocean floor near the Bermuda Triangle, which some interpret as the ruins of an ancient city. These claims, however, are often based on unverified or inconclusive evidence, and mainstream science has yet to find any proof of Atlantis or any other lost civilization beneath the waters of the Bermuda Triangle. Despite the lack of concrete evidence, the allure of Atlantis and its supposed connection to the Triangle continues to capture the imagination of those fascinated by ancient mysteries and hidden knowledge.

The idea of ghost ships and apparitions is another supernatural element frequently associated with the Bermuda Triangle. One of the most famous ghost ship stories linked to the Triangle is that of the *Mary Celeste*, a merchant ship found adrift in the Atlantic Ocean in 1872. While the *Mary Celeste* was discovered outside the traditional boundaries of the Bermuda Triangle, its eerie story has often been lumped into the Triangle's lore. When the ship was found, it was completely intact, with no signs of violence or struggle, yet its crew had vanished without a trace. Over the years, various supernatural explanations have been proposed, including the idea that the crew was abducted by ghosts or other paranormal entities. The *Mary Celeste* is not the only ghost ship associated with the Bermuda Triangle; there have been other reports of vessels found abandoned or drifting in the region, with no clear explanation for what happened to their crews.

In addition to ghost ships, there have been numerous reports of apparitions and strange lights within the Bermuda Triangle. Sailors and pilots have claimed to see phantom ships on the horizon or to witness strange glowing objects moving through the water or sky. Some of these sightings have been attributed to optical illusions caused by the ocean's reflective surface or the play of light on the water, but others remain unexplained. The idea of apparitions and ghostly figures is deeply rooted in maritime folklore, and the Bermuda Triangle, with its history of disappearances and unexplained events, provides fertile ground for such supernatural stories to thrive.

While the supernatural claims surrounding the Bermuda Triangle are intriguing and often entertaining, most scientists and skeptics remain unconvinced that there is anything otherworldly at play. They point to natural explanations for the disappearances, such as sudden storms, powerful ocean currents, human error, and mechanical failure. The Bermuda Triangle is located in a heavily trafficked area of the ocean, which increases the likelihood of accidents, and the region's unpredictable weather patterns can create dangerous conditions for ships and planes. Additionally, the Gulf Stream, a powerful ocean current that flows through the Triangle, can quickly disperse debris and wreckage, making it difficult to locate missing vessels.

One of the most commonly cited natural explanations for the strange occurrences in the Bermuda Triangle is methane hydrate eruptions from the ocean floor. Methane hydrates are gas deposits trapped beneath the seabed, and when they erupt, they can create massive bubbles that rise to the surface, reducing the water's density. This sudden change in buoyancy could cause ships to sink rapidly, without leaving much debris behind. While this theory is plausible, there is no direct evidence to suggest that methane hydrate eruptions are responsible for the disappearances in the Bermuda Triangle.

Another possible explanation is the presence of electromagnetic anomalies in the area. The Bermuda Triangle is known for causing compass malfunctions, and some theorists believe that this could be due to natural magnetic fields that interfere with navigation equipment. However, scientists have found no evidence of any unusual magnetic activity in the region that would be strong enough to cause planes or ships to vanish. Instead, they argue that any compass malfunctions are likely the result of human error or equipment failure.

In conclusion, while the supernatural claims surrounding the Bermuda Triangle are compelling and have become an integral part of its legend, there is little scientific evidence to support them. Theories of alien abductions, time warps, lost civilizations, and ghost ships may capture the imagination, but they remain speculative and unproven. Most experts agree that the disappearances and strange occurrences in the Bermuda Triangle can be explained by natural phenomena, such as extreme weather, powerful ocean currents, and human error. However, the enduring mystery of the Bermuda Triangle, combined with its rich history of strange tales, ensures that supernatural explanations will continue to play a role in the public's fascination with this enigmatic part of the world. The truth behind the supernatural claims may never be fully known, but as long as the Bermuda Triangle remains a place of intrigue and mystery, these theories will continue to captivate the minds of those who seek answers beyond the ordinary.

Epilogue

As our journey through the Bermuda Triangle comes to an end, we've uncovered a world where fact meets fiction and the line between the two often blurs. From the mysterious disappearances of ships and planes to the scientific theories that try to explain them, the Bermuda Triangle remains one of the most intriguing mysteries of our time.

But what have we learned? We've seen how natural forces like the Gulf Stream and strange weather patterns could play a role in the mysteries. We've explored the legends of ghost ships and lost civilizations, like Atlantis, that add a layer of wonder to this enigmatic region. And we've discovered that while some mysteries have logical explanations, others still leave us scratching our heads in wonder.

The Bermuda Triangle teaches us an important lesson: the world is full of unknowns, and sometimes, not having all the answers is what makes a mystery so captivating. It's a reminder that there's always more to explore, more to learn, and more to imagine.

So, as you close this book, remember that the adventure doesn't end here. The Bermuda Triangle, like many mysteries in our world, invites you to keep asking questions, to stay curious, and to never stop exploring. Who knows? Maybe one day, you'll be the one to unlock the secrets of the Bermuda Triangle—or perhaps, you'll uncover a new mystery of your own!

The End.